SKY SONGS

AMERICAN LIVES   *Series editor: Tobias Wolff*

SKY
SONGS

Meditations on Loving a Broken World   *Jennifer Sinor*

University of Nebraska Press | Lincoln

"Suppose Your Father Was a Redbird," by
Pattiann Rogers, originally appeared in *Firekeeper*
(Minneapolis MN: Milkweed Editions, 1994).
© Pattiann Rogers.

The essays in this collection were written over the
span of fifteen years. When referring to the Church of
Jesus Christ of Latter-day Saints and its members, the
author relies on the religious terminology, particularly
the forms of organizational identification, used and
promoted by the leadership of that institution at the
time each particular essay was written.

Library of Congress Cataloging-in-Publication Data
Names: Sinor, Jennifer, 1969– author.
Title: Sky songs: meditations on loving
a broken world / Jennifer Sinor.
Description: Lincoln: University of Nebraska
Press, [2020] | Series: American lives
Identifiers: LCCN 2020015706
ISBN 9781496222640 (paperback)
ISBN 9781496224026 (epub)
ISBN 9781496224033 (mobi)
ISBN 9781496224040 (pdf)
Subjects: LCSH: Sinor, Jennifer, 1969– |
Sinor, Jennifer, 1969–, —Family. | Utah—Biography.
Classification: LCC CT275.S521765 A3 2020 |
DDC 979.2—dc23
LC record available at
https://lccn.loc.gov/2020015706

Set in Garamond Premier Pro by
Mikala R. Kolander.
Designed by L. Auten.

For Aidan and Kellen

You who are the embodiment of blessing,
Once you know the way,
The nature of attention will call you to return.
Again and again, answer that call,
And be saturated with knowing,
"I belong here, I am at home."

Vijnana Bhairava Tantra
Translated by Lorin Roche

Contents

SKY SONGS

THE GROUND BELOW

Headwaters

For my father

For the first twelve hours after my father returned, his body still wrinkled from time spent immersed in water and wearing clothes that were three days old, he was under investigation for the murder of his brother. I imagine the questioning was only protocol for the rangers and the Fairbanks police; death in a national park requires the federal government to file a report whether that death is caused by a grizzly, an avalanche, or a body that just gives out. Still, I wonder if there was a moment in the police station, days away from the last time he had slept, his brother's body on its way to a temporary morgue, that my father's thoughts turned to questions of intention—his own or his brother's—and the ease with which a body can leave this earth.

The Alatna River headwaters, along with those of the Killik and Nigu Rivers, are found in the Gates of the Arctic National Park in northern Alaska, high up in the Brooks Range. One of six rivers in the national park designated "wild and scenic" and therefore federally protected, the river begins as a trickle and eventually builds to class III rapids on its eighty-three-mile journey to confluence with the Koyukuk. The park itself, over eight million acres of roadless, protected wilderness, is one of the most remote regions in the United States and home to the Arrigetch Peaks, with granitic spires that reach their fingers six thousand feet in the air, inspiring their Inupiat namesake, "fingers of hand outstretched." On the river one might see caribou, moose, Dall sheep, eagles, grizzly, and even the occasional seagull far from the shores of the Pacific.

Though the landscape can seem idyllic with its open tundra, boreal forests, and a river that snakes lazily across a valley floor, the Alatna has earned its "wild and scenic" designation. At the headwaters, the river is no more than a large drainage basin pooling in a barren lake named Summit. With little water, rafters beginning at Summit must drag their Avons for miles, over gravel bars and sand barriers, in hopes of finding a deeper channel. But the lack of water is deceiving. A little rain or an atypically hot day can cause a dramatic rise in the water level, as much as six feet at once, due to glacial melting or the refusal of the thick permafrost to absorb the rainfall. Within minutes, the river becomes a series of chutes, some as narrow as a canoe, where water rages down the mountain in search of the sea. Every guidebook, map, and website surveying the region reminds potential visitors that these rivers are ultimately unmappable.

My son was conceived the night my uncle died. Curling his body and holding fast to the slender strands of willow growing nearby, my uncle left this world on a day with no night, while the collection of cells that would become my son clung to the walls of my body, defying the odds and remaining viable. The following day, my uncle still dead and the cells still holding on and dividing, I whined in my journal about how quickly pens seem to lose their ink.

My father and his brother, Jerry, had gone to the northern reaches of Alaska to run the Alatna River for many reasons, some articulated and others unplumbed: because my uncle Jerry had run it before and knew no wilder place; because my dad never had and it was on Jerry's lifelist to return; because Alaska is enormous and unknown, a land with a history that trembles on the page, and therefore a place worthy of reckoning; because Jerry was sick and his time spent on trails and in tents was becoming limited; and, perhaps, because Alaska hovered like a dream from their childhood, when they would spend long afternoons in the hayloft listening to the mice scurry along the floorboards while they scanned the reaches of the landlocked plains and considered what lay beyond.

Written first on a legal pad in thin blue lines of ink that run like waves across the page, then later transferred to a computer, the journal my dad made of the trip, composed on the flight back, begins:

Jerry and I met in St. Louis to begin our incredible journey.

He then moves quickly to describe those first few hours—not even twenty-four—when everything was still okay. Arriving in Fairbanks, flying to the hinterlands, renting gear from the out-fitter, he names the few people they met, the meals they ate, the conversations they had with the taxi driver. I imagine his pen pausing for lengths of time as he begins the story, nursing the drink the flight attendant gave him moments before, staring into the clouds, and willing himself to recall more of what would typically pass unnoticed, not wanting to set out on the next leg of the journey, one he knows will lead to pain. I imagine he clings to these opening moments the way, in the river, he clung to their raft, and is frightened when he must leave them behind. Yet he begins.

My dad is a storyteller. When I was a child, he would tuck me in at night with a story conjured from the air rather than the row of books lining the cabinet in the hall. He spun epic tales of three kids lost at sea who sailed on a houseboat and beat pirates, storms, and ocean swells that threatened to overtake them. The orphaned children fought fires and slew dragons by relying on their wits and always remained alive for the next adventure. As an adult, I imagine that these were the stories my dad created as a child and shared with his older brother, Jerry, while they walked to school or milked the cows. That in fact the tales had accompanied him his entire life.

Each night when the story was done, my dad would lie beside me, waiting for me to fall asleep. In the darkness, I would match my breathing to his, feeling my chest move in and out more quickly than usual, trying to stay awake longer than he could and always failing.

While the details of the stories he told me as a child have faded—I can no longer remember what the children actually spent their days doing or how it was they came to be orphaned—the power of language to make the world remains with me. Spinning the air itself, my father populated my bedroom with characters and adventures that followed me into my dreams. Even after he slipped from the bed and crept out of my room, I was not alone.

By the time my dad begins the second page of his journal, the ordinary has faded like fog with the rising sun. Well into the morning of their first day in the Alaskan wilderness, long after the bush pilot has left them at Summit Lake, he writes that Jerry fell while trying to fish. It is the first glimmer. After recording the number of fish Jerry catches, their length and type, he writes that Jerry told him he had fallen while walking back to the camp and was worried he maybe cracked a rib. In among the Arctic char comes a hint, like frost, of fragility.

As though falling were not worrisome enough, on the morning of the second day, they realize that fuel is running low. My dad does not write why, but I know it is because my uncle overhauled the fuel canisters before they left and did a poor job. The irony is bitter, for my uncle was a chemical engineer, a specialist, in fact, in fuels. The founder and editor of what became the *Sinor Synthetic Fuels Report Quarterly*, he helped design the first space shuttle in the '80s, worked on alternative fuel sources in the '90s, and finds himself, on July 12, 2003, faced with the knowledge that he and his brother are two days into a fourteen-day trip and have already used half of their fuel.

Aidan has not yet been conceived on July 12. His being waits in the universe for a body, and in my journal I remain transfixed by the ordinary in my life: a new puppy that won't behave, a deadline for an essay, heat that has clamped the Intermountain West and refused to let go. I mow the lawn, riding the tractor up and down the hill beside our house, and consider calling my mom to make sure my dad has gotten off okay. In my journal I spend a page saying I have nothing to write about.

My husband, Michael, and I begin the day by painting the sun porch. By noon the heat is more than we can take, and we abandon the project for the cooler reaches of our living room. The day before my father left for Alaska, I chose not to call him to wish him a safe journey. Our last interaction, an argument over a card game, had left me angry and resentful, feelings as familiar and worn as my favorite shoes. I won't learn of their ordeal for several days. When I do, I will, at the age of thirty-four, believe that I am somehow to blame for the accident because I failed to call.

My dad and Jerry spend that afternoon falling as they struggle in inch-deep water and use ropes to line, or drag, the raft down the shallow headwaters of the Alatna. It is hard work, lining a boat. I say this not from experience but from the way my father's hands looked when he returned from Alaska—swollen and scabbed. The waters of the Alatna seemed to have pooled in his body. In fact, his hands were so bloated that my mother had to type the initial draft of his journal. The keys on the keyboard were too small. His hands betrayed the difficulty of the trip in a way his words never will, their stretched skin remaining with me later when he suggests that he did nothing at all.

Others had been asked to come along on the trip, including Michael and me. Being in the backcountry was something my extended family did together, like others might see a movie or eat out. Every summer we backpacked in the Rockies, choosing wilderness areas over national parks or forests in hopes that the additional work of trekking there would mean having part of the planet to ourselves. While a dozen people from three generations around a campfire in the Mount Zirkel Wilderness was not unusual for us, only two in the central Brooks Range was.

That second evening Jerry admits to my father that he had to lie to his doctor about coming on this trip. His prostate cancer and Parkinson's were becoming more complicated and he had, just days before, been placed on new medication that was giving him trouble. My dad writes:

> After dinner, we sat around the fire talking about successes and failures, investment strategies, future trips, hopes for our children and life in general. It was a very good evening, but it was also the first time he mentioned a third member of our group (Cynde) and [wondered] why she wasn't with us. When I said, "Cynde did not come on this trip." He responded, "I know, I just forgot."

Crystal clear in thought only forty-eight hours ago, Jerry now confuses white rocks for sand dollars and imagines people who aren't there. Reeling my mother, Cynde, into the story, my uncle's mind seeks refuge in the familiar, as she typically accompanied them on their trips. In fact she was on their last trip to Alaska when the same river, the Alatna, had pulled her under with its giant river arms, leaving her bruised and sore but not broken.

Reading this as a warning, she chose not go on this trip—the cold, the mosquitoes, the lack of dry land. We all found excuses; mine had something to do with a porch that needed to be painted and a new dog that couldn't be left alone. When we learn that Jerry is dead, when we learn that my dad has, by himself, paddled the body of his dead brother for nearly a hundred miles in search of help, we will wonder, with Jerry, why we weren't there.

Jerry, though, refuses to allow us to remain outside the warmth of the campfire and brings us into the story—first my mother then, the following day, his daughter, his wife, his son, and others—weaving us into the landscape. Perhaps he imagines my mother gone for a minute to the tent to put on a layer of fleece, or his daughter down by the river watching for eagles, or his son on a night hike, waiting for stars that will never appear. For Jerry, it seems, we are all there in Alaska, poking a stick at the coals in the campfire as the night declines to come to an end and the sun lingers forever on the horizon.

Because I am the oldest in my family, I cannot say what it is like to have an older sibling, one whom, perhaps, you have revered your entire life, whose path you have followed, whose choices you have been taught to see as good and right, and whose decline you must witness. Instead, I am familiar with the responsibility of being the eldest, of making a path, of always being watched. I know, I just forgot, says Jerry, the one who never failed his siblings or his children. My first thoughts are how hard that moment must be for two men born in the Corn Belt just after the Depression, when fragility and error simply were not options. I imagine the shifting of feet, the stoking of fire, the busying of hands with mess kits and fishing line, anything to ignore the monster that has crept into camp, threatening to disrupt a pattern, a practiced way of being, that these two men have lived for over sixty years.

But later, I reconsider this moment in my dad's story. My dad reads the early signs of mental deterioration in Jerry's inability to distinguish between reality and figment, but I wonder if the dementia is not working to refigure a truer truth, the emotional truth of things. What if Jerry's failing mind is only failing to erect the boundaries and borders we typically build, and the possibility exists that those who are not "there" are actually there. What if it feels as if others are warming themselves by the fire and the felt truth is the actual truth. What if, rather than being alone in the Alaskan wilds without fuel and with physical and mental loss pressing in, my dad and his brother are actually surrounded by family, a fact that only Jerry understands and registers in the story he tells.

Or maybe I am just wishing it were so. Maybe Jerry doesn't feel grace in the dissolving line between fact and fiction but rather experiences the swirling hysteria that must accompany a declining grip on reality. Maybe when he says, I know, I know, he is really wishing with all his heart to stand firmly on the banks of reality.

I will not know that I am pregnant for several weeks. Only Aidan will know of his existence and then only in a cellular way. That I could be inhabited by another without my knowledge unnerves me. Hormones busily make preparations for my body to do what it has never been taught but must somehow now do, and I open another carton of milk for my breakfast cereal. In my journal I worry that friends no longer like me, that I am achieving nothing this summer, that I want to back out of a conference in September, that I should call my mom but don't. All the while an egg is waiting and a favorite uncle dying.

When I look back at these entries years later, days where I know my dad was fighting to stay alive, I am at first embarrassed by what fills the page. Though I could not know of the miracles happening around me, I wish I had been less concerned about the mundane and more outwardly focused. I find it hard to imagine that I could write several lines about the inadequacy of my pen and the failures of an eight-week-old puppy. More recently, though, I have begun to see these pages as a kind of tether, a line connecting me to these ordinary moments in my past, allowing me to recover what would have typically been left to fade. On July 14, 2003, hormones releasing, my father fighting, and my uncle failing, I worried about taking our new puppy running. To have left this moment unwritten would have severed the only connection I have to a day in my life where the world split open without my notice.

Day three is, my dad writes with typical understatement, a difficult day. By late morning, Jerry can no longer stand upright. As long as he keeps walking, he can remain erect, but as soon as he stops moving, he falls into the river, the raft, the rocks on the shore. The Alatna is painfully dry. My dad and uncle continue to line the fifteen-foot Avon down the shallows and over the sand and gravel bars, heaving their belongings, wishing for more water. Rain falls. Granitic rock formations appear in the far distance, holding court above the U-shaped valley while nothing on the valley floor grows above a foot—tussocks, sedge, and the occasional willow, beaten low by a wind that hammers the landscape. Every now and then, an eagle flies overhead, a herd of caribou flee their approach, the rains desist for a minute, and the sky opens. Every now and then, my uncle asks where they are and where everyone else is. When this happens, my dad responds, Jerry, we are in the middle of Alaska going down the Alatna and there are only two of us.

Only two.

Only two days ago, all was right in the world. Two years ago, the signs of Parkinson's were less apparent. Two decades ago, they were in the prime of life building shuttles that could return to earth and writing treaties dictating how the world should act in times of war. Two score ago, they were getting married, finishing school, taking road trips to Florida to see the alligators. Only two.

More falling. One moment my dad looks up and Jerry is gone. Beaching the raft, he goes in search of his brother only to find him near the shoreline, soaking wet; gloves, glasses, hat gone. He was looking for my mother in the cottongrass. She has been absent so long. Time bends like the river. Now and then, here and there, near and far move closer together. I am at home writing in my journal an entry that will forever root me to this day long after the day has passed, the egg that will become my son knits into my body either to grow or to perish, and over a campfire the night before, my dad and his brother bring us onto the river in the stories they tell.

Though he only admits "real concern" at this point, there must be terror for my father, who is two hundred miles away from a city of any size with a brother who is gradually leaving him. He searches for the missing gloves and hat and then abandons the search. Who knows what the river might have taken. Is it at this point, I wonder, with so much missing and surrounded by acres of tundra, that he remembers a conversation he had with Jerry shortly after his Parkinson's diagnosis. Knowing that the disease would leave him bedridden and imprisoned in a body that at one point could bushwhack through the Rockies for miles without rest, Jerry asked his younger brother to make sure he died in the natural world. When the time came, to help him find a cliff, a valley, a bottomless river, a final ceiling of sky. Using the raft to steady Jerry's failing body and guiding both down a river that is no longer shallow but has grown steadily in the rain and the lower elevation, perhaps my father turns to the now clear sky and considers what he is being asked to do.

They set up camp, my dad erecting Jerry's tent, and eat a cold dinner. The lighters and the waterproof matches were soaked during the day's struggles and will not light. Somehow the plastic bag has been left open. My dad's account does not have to mention that Jerry was in charge of these things—more than ten years of backpacking with my extended family tells me that Jerry held the matches. He was the one who made the fire, cooked the food, called us from our tents when the sun was just beginning to chase away the morning chill. He was the one who chose the routes, found the campsite, told us how close to the river we could pitch our tents. He was the one who held the map, named the stars, and warned us repeatedly about the three greatest threats in wilderness backpacking: lightning, sunstroke, and falling.

Day four. Jerry can no longer speak. His voice is a whisper, words slurring together. They decide over breakfast that they are in real trouble and need to head for help at Takahula Lake, a journey of sixty miles. Two retired school teachers live in a remote cabin in the woods near the lake with their dog and a satellite phone, information handed to them with their fishing licenses and now more precious than fuel.

This, then, is the way things are. My dad writes, Jerry was gone part of the time. In these moments, he is utterly alone.

The last time I saw my uncle was only a week or so before the Alaska trip. We had a Sinor family reunion in Grand Island, Nebraska. My dad's younger brother, Keith, lives on a lake and the family gathered for a weekend of swimming and boating and beach picnics. The entire family was there, uncles and aunts, nieces and nephews, brothers and sisters sweating under the midwestern sun while the black flies bit our ankles.

On the first morning of the reunion, I took a picture of my uncle and his family, the camera holding what would soon be lost. They were dressed in blue and stood in the shade. It is the intimacy of that moment, their bodies touching at the elbows, our eyes meeting through the lens, that I remember. All of us, for a fraction of time, holding the pose and each other.

Jerry was very thin. While his no-fat diet gave his prostate cancer little to invade, it left his body with little to live upon. Each time I saw him his belt was cinched tighter, his clothes hanging more loosely from his limbs. Yet, he seemed strong. We all said so, standing around the food tables, eating potato salad, watching him play badminton. Yes, we assured ourselves, he was well despite the drugs, the treatments, the long slide to immobility that is Parkinson's.

When the thunderstorm came, we all ran for the garage, bringing beach chairs and the leftover food with us. All of us, except Jerry. He headed in the opposite direction, to the lake, where waves were competing with each other to touch the sky. A few minutes later, we saw him push off from the boat dock on the jet ski and ride to the center of the lake where he began whirling in tight circles as the lightening and the thunder came down. We only pointed. Rain hit the tin roof like hail, making it impossible to hear one another. In my mind's eye, he raises his fist to the storm and transgresses, for a moment, his own mortality. He demands participation in life. He will not remain off stage for the drama. The lightning does not strike him down, and he grows in my eyes.

Remembering how this once thick man rode a jet ski like a weapon a week before he died, I recall also a moment of fragility in a small hotel near Lake Titicaca, our final day in Peru. We were all there: my brother, his wife, my mom and dad, Michael, my aunt, Jerry, his daughter, and her husband, a group that typically fished together every summer, now staying in a motel that bordered the world's highest navigable lake. Because Jerry wanted to see Machu Picchu before he died, we spent our frequent flyer miles, hired a guide to take us on the Inca Trail, and found ourselves a year before his death exploring the city of Cusco, the belly button of the world.

The trip was amazing, but tiring. Tiring for all of us. The altitude, the constant travel, the food, the water. We were weathered. On the last day, we were gathering our suitcases and backpacks one last time. Ivan, our guide, was trying to hustle us out of the hotel and into the van that would take most of us, eventually, back to Lima and our flight home. There was a chance we would miss the plane. The commotion—eleven adults trying to load themselves into a van, some of us staying longer, some leaving that night, others the next day—filled the tiny lobby of the hotel and bounced against the low ceiling and narrow door. Amid the chaos, Jerry came into the lobby, unsteady like a child, eyes wide in alarm. Ivan, Ivan, he said, his voice matching the shakiness of his limbs, I have lost my tickets.

We stopped, all of us, bags half zipped, empty water bottles limp at our sides, and looked to Jerry—the man whose knowledge and experience had seemed as boundless as space itself—willing him with our eyes not to be fragile. Please, I thought, please do not show me this tender part of your belly. I do not want to know that you are anything except what you have ever been. I do not want you to be anything but whole.

And in my silent willing, I refused him his humanity.

Day four still. Afternoon. Latitude 67°44' north. The GPS places them, roots them to a locatable spot on the spinning globe, but they are far from still. They start the raft down a narrow chute. Rainfall, permafrost, and the many small creeks that run into the Alatna have conspired to create a torrent. Water rushes them headlong down the river, sweepers leaning like animals of prey, ready to pull them from the raft and send them into the roils. When they turn the corner and see the giant shale outcrop, a wall of rock that cuts across the chute, they can do nothing but slam into it. The raft buckles and climbs the wall; my dad, in front, is thrown out of the raft and pulled under the outcrop. Somehow the raft too goes under or around or over. No one knows. When my dad comes up for air, Jerry and the raft are also on the other side.

The bottom of the Avon has been shredded but miraculously neither my dad nor Jerry are seriously injured. They decide to camp for the night while they try to repair the raft with duct tape. Jerry repeatedly suggests that they just walk to the car and go home. Unable to stand at all, Jerry gathers wood on his hands and knees in hopes of building a fire to warm my father.

That night Jerry insists that they find their location on the GPS. My dad argues, seeing no point in knowing their latitude and longitude when their only choice is to head south on the river, but Jerry will not surrender the point. Finally, my dad agrees and they find the coordinates of the camp. These will also be the coordinates of Jerry's death.

I wonder at Jerry's insistence. Is it, in a sense, the final act of caretaking in a life dedicated to securing the safety of others, of making sure there is order in the world before leaving it? Or is it because he feels at some deep level that a final resting place should be a known place, a place that holds itself, in its specificity, its repeatability, against the vastness that is the Alaskan wilds, the vastness of the universe? Or is it because his mind, cast to sea, unable to latch on to anyone or anything long enough to recover rationality, holds the GPS like a flotation device, willing the linear to return? For whatever reason, Jerry insists, and because of his insistence, we, as a family, will be able to return someday to that shore, to those willows, to those rocks, and stand in the thicket where he lay down to die.

My dad helps Jerry get ready for bed, dressing him in his long johns and tucking him into his sleeping bag, as he did for me as a child, perhaps as Jerry once did for him. Hours later, from his own tent, my dad hears Jerry struggling with the zipper on his tent. What are you doing, he asks. And Jerry responds that he wants to try his new fly line. The first coherent words in over a day, my dad takes it as a sign that the drugs are kicking in. Go to bed, he says. And this time, when my dad lies down to sleep, it is the sleep of release. Things will be okay, he tells himself. The drugs are working.

In the predawn hours of July 15, my dad hears Jerry struggle again with the zipper on his tent. When he goes over and asks Jerry what he is doing, Jerry responds, What are you doing here? My dad repeats the question; Jerry repeats the answer. Unlike all the other times in which my dad has explained that they are in the middle of Alaska trying to make it home and Jerry has responded that he knows that but had just forgotten, this time Jerry never returns to the here. He remains there, wherever there is, and wonders what my dad is doing at his side.

When the sun comes up, Jerry is gone.

My dad spends two hours looking for him, following his footprints, worrying that he has tried to go fishing and been pulled into the Alatna. But fishing was not what Jerry had in mind. Jerry's boot tracks lead north and west of their tents, meandering for close to fifty yards, until they stop near the river. At the end of the trail, my father finds his brother curled up like a baby in a thicket of willows some yards from the river. Jerry has been careful to lie down next to the willows rather than on them, sharing the ground, choosing a place. Sometime in the night he reached into his dry bag, to the very bottom, and put on his "going home" clothes, the clean shirt and pants meant for the plane ride back. Earlier in the evening, he could not zip his tent. Now he has laced his own boots. Clothes clean, no sign of a fall or struggle, he is holding a small branch in his hand, holding it like you might a walking stick.

My dad, who must serve simultaneously as brother, oarsman, and priest, blesses the land and loads the boat. In this story, only one of the heroes lives to see another day. I know my father well enough to know that such an ending is unacceptable.

Jerry was diagnosed with Parkinson's in 1995. The following August the Sinor family backpack was in Mount Zirkel. It was the first backpack since Jerry's diagnosis and the first since my divorce. Loss, it seems, is democratic.

That we would both carry on with our lives was never a question. His illness and my failed marriage did not even warrant conversation. No one said anything to either of us. We hiked, fished, and ate as we always had. Around the campfire we talked about books, or legal questions, or politics, or what the fish seemed to be biting this year. At times I wanted to scream, hold out my emptiness like an amputated limb and demand it be acknowledged, but instead I stirred the soup in my cup and waited for it to cool.

That is, until the last day. We were breaking camp for the final climb out to the cars. Everyone was busy stuffing backpacks, filtering water, or laying ground cloths in the sun to dry. My aunt and I were folding the tent that I had shared in the past with my husband. We were absorbed in one of the greatest pleasures of backpacking—the economy with which you travel, the fact that each thing has its own place—and all seemed fine.

I looked over at Jerry, who was busy attending to his own possessions as well as those of the community. At this point in time, he looked as he had always looked. But then so did I. To anyone else, we were the same. I walked over to him.

What I said was, I am sorry that you have Parkinson's. What I meant was thank you for taking me into the natural world and showing me how mountains rest their tired bodies against one another and rivers scrape out plains the size of entire states, how meteors return like swallows every year in August to flash across the sky and wildflowers fill valleys so that you can no longer see the trail. What I meant was that I hoped he would find peace, that he would always be able to recognize himself, that he would not be in pain. What I meant was that I felt like I was a failure because John left me, that sometimes when I sat very still on my couch at home loneliness suffocated me, that I could not understand how things would ever feel okay again. What I meant was that I was scared. What I meant was that I would bear witness to his loss in hopes that he would bear witness to mine.

After securing my uncle's body in the Avon, my dad pushes off from the shore. Over the next sixty miles, he is thrown from the raft some thirty or forty times, in each instance fearing he will lose the raft, his brother's body, his only way home. Sand bars catch him and roll his body across their stretches, wearing holes in his neoprene waders and gloves and plunging him repeatedly into ice-cold water. A night and a day pass. Finally, after wandering for miles in the woods, he finds the cabin with the satellite phone.

About pushing off from the site where Jerry died, my dad writes, By luck, not by plan, Jerry was facing me for the rest of the trip.

With no one else to talk to and a river that seemed to wish them gone, my father turns one last time to his brother for support and begins to talk. For close to two days, he paddles, swims, climbs, falls, and tells stories. Perhaps he recalls moments from their childhood, throwing rocks over the barn, swimming in the irrigation ditch, the taste of tomatoes fresh from the vine. Perhaps he thanks Jerry for going to college and showing his siblings another way of being in the world, for giving my father a different life than he had ever imagined while inoculating pigs and driving the tractor through corn. Perhaps he describes the scenery as they move from tundra into boreal forests, into the winking greens of the white and black spruce. I know he sang songs, and I know my father well enough to know that when he forgot the words to "Tom Dooley" or "John Henry," he made them up, fanciful songs about heroes and lovers and trains that go all night. I know my father told Jerry he loved him.

In his journal he writes, *we* talked, blurring once again the boundary between here and there. And for this I am grateful. Because when I think of what my father went through, what it would have been like to make the trip to Takahulu, the only comfort I can take is in knowing my father had company. As he had several nights before over the campfire, my dad brings all of us onto the raft, a raft on which Jerry is not dead and they are not alone. Weaving together stories of the past, he creates a net that holds all of us, a net that carries him to safety, to home.

The morning my father arrives at Takahulu Lake, I write in my journal that I am going rafting in two days down the Snake River. Worried that the time away from my desk is time poorly spent, I imagine writing an essay about the experience, what it is like to float down a river that begins in the mountains and runs to the sea. Mostly I complain about the dog and how easily I am distracted by household projects. Still, this is the last entry I have before I learn of Jerry's death, the last recorded narrative of what my life was like when Jerry was alive, my father whole, and my son the size of a period.

I like to imagine that at the very moment Jerry slipped the ropes that bind us to this planet, my son Aidan was conceived, so that for the briefest of moments, the past, present, and future stood together and recognized one another. I like to imagine that the suffering my dad experienced, pain that has haunted him every day since his return, is measured out among us, so that we all carry part of the burden. I like to imagine that the stories I tell here, like the stories my dad told me as a child and the ones he recited as a way to remain sane on the river, have the power to reach across distance, and time, and death and connect me to him, and him to Jerry, and Jerry to Aidan. Jerry can no longer tell his story, and I must carry Aidan's for him until he is older. Someday he will carry mine, and I will tell my father's, and loss will be found in language.

Where It Is Darkest

We awake to a skiff of snow still on the ground, the temperature barely above ten. Outside our window, darkness conceals the newly bare branches of the maple in front of our house, and stars linger in the sky. Michael is sick with a stomachache. He has been up all night, tossing and turning, flipping his pillow every so often to find the cool side. Nothing seems to help. Around three in the morning, I found him curled into a ball on the bathroom floor, the terra-cotta tiles surrounding him like a field aflame.

Now, I leave him in bed wrapped to his chin in the down comforter and head out for a run. It is Tuesday, two days before Thanksgiving and a day we teach at the university thirty-five miles from our house. We are up early. My running route takes me along the foothills of the Bear Mountains under a sky threaded with falling stars. Because we live in the country, well away from even the small city of Logan, Utah, the darkness is complete. I have no idea where each footfall will land and trust the road is beneath me.

As I run, I think of Michael home in bed in our house that sits across the fields. Growing up, my mother told me I could will away sickness. "Just tell yourself you're not sick," she would say, standing over my bed in the morning, her eyes on me but her mind chasing down the day. Her tone was the same she used when she would tell me to imagine a field of flowers when I awoke from a nightmare. That a monster inevitably burst from the dancing poppies, jaw open, mouth drooling, and seized my seven-year-old body suggested a lack of control on my part. "You're not trying hard enough." The body, my body, was something I could master. Thirty-some years from childhood, I push my body hard. My mother's unswerving belief in mind over matter urges me to rise every morning, even now, four months pregnant, and run six miles along country roads long before the sun crowns the mountains and illuminates the broken stalks of corn.

Instead of checking on Michael when I return from my run, I head straight for the bathroom, gloves still on, frost melting at the tips of my hair. The furnace ignites when I flip the light switch, pushing warm air to my feet. At the toilet, I pull down my underwear. They are clean, no blood.

Every baby book I have read indicates you can continue your regular exercise routine while pregnant. However, when listing what those activities might include the authors name walking, yoga, or swimming, never a six-mile run every morning at an elevation where oxygen is scarce. The absence of pregnant women running across the pages of the baby books suggests I am already a bad mother before I have even become one. On morning runs, I have taken to wearing Michael's jacket to hide my growing belly from the neighbors. The worry that I could lose the baby through such strenuous exercise does not trump the need to test my strength. Pregnancy has become just one more factor that proves my dedication to endurance, not unlike running in below-zero weather or while lightning strikes nearby.

On the drive south, Michael at home, a bottle of Pepto-Bismol within his reach, I imagine running this stretch of highway, cresting this hill, feeling the road curve beneath me. The lack of a shoulder means that few run this four-lane road. Cars speed past at close to sixty. One slip means death, especially in the winter when snowplowed mounds of muddied snow narrow the road.

When I was a child, I ran without fear. I used to head out every night after dinner with my father to run a long, slow loop that circled our military housing area. We met soldiers in white T-shirts and jangling dog tags who nodded to my father as we passed. At the end of our run, I would race my father up the last hill, feet pounding the pavement, a whirl of motion. Every stride made me think I might fly.

My mother may or may not have had a miscarriage in Italy in the summer of 1967. The fact that I don't know indicates how little we talk about compromised bodies in my family. Something happened that summer, halfway through my parents' yearlong trip around the world, and an emergency room in Rome was required. When describing their year abroad, they focus on the man in India beating chapatti on his bare thighs or how they smuggled Mao's red book out of China. Rome itself is a black hole; the story always stops in Italy. "We had to find a hospital," my father says, and in the silence that follows I imagine a sea of blood.

Miscarriage lurks in my past—there's my mother sweating in the black hole of Rome, my great aunt as well, and even my great, great, great aunt, a willowy woman who kept a diary while homesteading in the Dakotas in the late nineteenth century. Though she too does not speak of such loss head on. Rather she codes those moments in the pages of her diary, the months where her period stops only to return again, four months later, along with ruined loaves of bread and snow that doesn't end.

None of us speaks of a moment when our bodies failed. Instead, I lace my running shoes, don a baggy jacket, and set out in single-digit Fahrenheit, the cold freezing the liquid that pools in the corners of my eyes, exhalations frozen into a grizzled beard from ear to chin.

"Something's really wrong," Michael says when I call home after my first class. "My stomach hurts so much. It's like I swallowed glass." His voice sounds tired and thin, as if pressed between rocks. Earlier in the morning, I had thought he was being weak in not going to work, knew I would have chosen differently, but now I am worried.

My return drive north takes close to forty minutes, and I spend much of it on the phone telling Michael how close I am: through Smithfield, past Lewiston, over the border into Idaho, sweeping by the Cub River. When not talking with him, I call my parents. Hearing the panic in my voice, my mother thinks I am the sick one. She asks again and again how I feel. The first time my mother has uttered the word "miscarriage" aloud, it makes me immediately recall my morning run. It's as if she had sped to the bathroom with me, waited while I pulled my running tights and underwear to my knees. Palpably relieved when she learns Michael's stomach, not mine, is cramping, she hands the phone to my father.

From six hundred miles away my father, who is not a doctor, diagnoses appendicitis and explains the test I can do when I arrive home, something about pushing my fingers into his abdomen and then releasing. His belly should hurt either more or less either before or after or during. I can't think well enough to remember. Ten minutes later, sitting by Michael in the bed, I will push on his stomach but learn nothing.

When I was in high school, my family stationed for the third time near Pearl Harbor, a serial killer began murdering young women on the Pali Highway. From the local swap meet, he had purchased a flashing blue light that he displayed on his dashboard just like Steve McGarrett on *Hawaii Five-O*. Wearing the stolen uniform of a police officer, the man stopped women on the highway. Those two props—the whirling light and the uniform—were enough to lure victim after victim from her car and into the dark and viny kudzu along the road to be raped and killed.

I drove the Pali regularly because my boyfriend lived on the Windward side of the island, and I often drove at night. As young woman after young woman slipped from this world in a bloody and violent way, my dad became more aggressive in his advice. At first I was only to keep the window rolled up if the police ever stopped me. Soon, though, he was telling me never to stop for anyone, including the police, just to drive to the nearest police station and take the matter up there. If all else failed he said, if for some reason I found myself out of the car and in danger, I must use my legs and run. "They are your best weapon," he told me. I could outrun anyone.

Here is what I learn about pain while we wait for the doctor to arrive in the emergency room at the nearby rural hospital. The more it hurts, the deeper a person descends into himself. Michael lies on the examining table in agony. He doesn't cry, doesn't howl, but rather moans softly to himself. His eyes remain closed, the color bleeds from his skin leaving him transparent, and he retreats into his body.

"Can't he have some medicine?" I say to every nurse, every Sally-Carrie-Ashley who comes into the room and takes his temperature, his blood pressure, his pulse. "Can't you give him something for the pain?"

Every time they talk about lab results and doctors and all the reasons we must wait.

"He's strong," I say to them. "He never complains about pain. He really needs help."

Nothing.

When he throws up all over both of us, I point to my splattered boots as evidence of the severity of the situation when Sally-Carrie-Ashley passes through the room again. "Do you see?" I say. "He's not making this up." An odd thing to say given the fact that his white blood cell count has skyrocketed and his arms tremble in pain. I hear my mother in my words. The nurse only calls for cleanup.

An hour later, the technicians position Michael for an X-ray, opening his curled form and exposing the belly he has been holding for hours. The pain grows so great that I think Michael has fainted. He goes limp, yellows, his eyes roll back. I want to hit someone, shake them awake, put their face to Michael's clenched hands and sockless feet and make them look. Seemingly unaware of what is happening, the technicians swing the giant arm of the X-ray machine over Michael's stomach and leave the gun-like end hovering above his body. Michael whimpers, stretched open, flattened to the ceiling and beyond that, the sky. At that moment, I no longer want drugs, or doctors, or a hospital taller than one floor. What I want is to take Michael's suffering into my own body and carry it along with the baby whose presence, up until now, has felt vague and unknown. Faced with loss, that weight suddenly feels more certain.

Instead I wait for the results like I might a coffee, hands folded, purse at my side.

At eighth grade graduation, I received the award for perfect attendance. I hadn't missed a day of school, the only student in my class honored with such a distinction. While most that age would have preferred being named "most popular," I took a peculiar pride in my certificate. I thought it indicated strength, that I could conquer anything if I put my mind to it. After all, that is what my mother told me in the morning when I complained of a headache. "The mind's a powerful thing," she would say, sending me to school with an aspirin. I learned to believe her, taped my award to the wall above my bed.

When I outgrew the age of certificates, when attendance was no longer taken, I became a runner, my own personal check mark each morning, six miles, all before sun up, in blizzards, in deserts, in air thin as rice paper. I never missed a day, no matter what was happening in my life, an early meeting, a hurt knee, a growing baby in my uterus. Days when I woke sick, a runny nose or a cough, I felt especially strong to be running in two-degree blackness.

They find a troubling spot on the X-ray and decide to send Michael by ambulance to the bigger hospital in Logan thirty-five miles away. For the trip, the doctor orders an IV with morphine. When the nurse arrives, I am heady with relief. Morphine. Strong stuff. What they once gave soldiers on the battlefield before cutting off an arm or a leg. The nurse sticks him no fewer than five times trying to find a vein. At one point she hits the bone in his wrist with the needle, and Michael's body leaps from the table as if electrocuted.

"You're hurting him," I cry, after his body settles back down. "Can't we find someone else?"

The nurse and I look around the small room at the shine of steel and glass. We are alone. Her eyes fail to meet mine, and she returns to tapping his forearm as if transmitting code. Ensnared by my own misery, I never once consider the one who holds the needle.

Michael chooses the pain over being stuck again, refuses the morphine. On that note, we leave the Preston hospital, but not before I plow head-on into a door that appears out of nowhere. It is then that I begin to cry.

Hours later, now at the Cache Valley Specialty Hospital in Logan, I am documenting what has happened in a tiny purple journal my friend Kelli brought me along with a grocery sack full of food. She has purchased peanut butter that I can squeeze onto crackers, which takes me back to childhood and the morning snacks my mother made for me. Each bite, each snap of salt mingling with sweet swirls of peanut butter, reminds me of a time in life when someone else recognized my hunger long before I did. They have given Michael Demerol mixed with Phenergan, the latter a medicine that coursed through his veins like fire, burning from the inside out. It took several more attempts to insert the IV, but now he sleeps. The CAT scans have revealed a blockage between his small and large intestine, what the doctor called "an obstruction in his bowels." Something deep inside him, in the body's darkest, most interior space. Nobody can explain how it got there.

At 9:30 p.m., after a day filled with pain and unknowing, I hold Michael's hand as several nurses push a thick tube up Michael's nose, down his throat, and into his stomach. His body does everything to reject the tube, throat tightening, jaw clenching, hands flailing in the air. The nurses try twice and finally succeed in inserting the NG tube. Michael falls back against his pillow, breathing roughly, and I fight competing desires to flee or to make my stand and scream.

That night I sleep on a cot near his bed. I hold my stomach and cry, worried that this baby I am carrying will be born without a father, worried I will miscarry under all the stress, awaken in a field of my own blood. For so long I have been concerned about the physical stress on my body produced by running, the pounding, the jostling, the competition for air, but now I fear emotional strain.

No one to talk to, no one to call, at 11:30 Michael wakes up crying, "Oh, Jennifer. God. I can't stand it. Can't stand it." I hold his hand, rubbing his wrists carefully to avoid the bruises that have resulted from the repeated attempts to insert the IV. "I'll ask for more medicine," I say. Outside the window, pitch black.

One morning when I was running, maybe three years after we had moved to Cache Valley, I was startled by a skunk scurrying along the brushy edge of the road. Far from uncommon, skunks often appeared along my running route just when night lifted the hem of her skirts from the hills. That morning, thin light was already weaving through the fields, touching each alfalfa stem. The skunk surprised me, but I was more taken by its strange actions. Rather than dart back into the long grasses at the sound of my approach, he rambled along the edge of the road, taking in the morning colors with little fear.

While I was busy thinking about how lucky I was to live in a place where wild things emerge from the grasses to scuttle at my feet, a small truck pulled up alongside me. If it had been darker or if I were living somewhere besides rural Idaho, I might have worried at the slowing of a vehicle. In this case, though, I just kept running, leaving the skunk and the truck, assuming those in the cab had also stopped to marvel at the wonders offered by this world.

I had gone a hundred yards when I heard the gunshots: four of them, puncturing the morning stillness. Without thought, I stopped and turned, trying to see my way back through the silt of dawn. Two men had gotten out of the truck and were on the side of the road, but the truck's headlights prevented me from seeing anything else.

I debated what to do. Tired and with only a mile and a half to go, I realized I wasn't sure I wanted to know what was happening back at the truck. It seemed easier to ignore the situation, mind my own business, pretend that gun shots punctuated all my runs. Perhaps because I had only moments ago been thinking how happy that skunk made me, or perhaps because the skunk reminded me of what I love about living here, I ran back.

By the time I arrived, the two men were already inside the cab and starting to drive away. I stood in the middle of the road, hoping they would stop. In my running shorts and T-shirt, I felt small and exposed and for a moment second-guessed my decision.

"What are you doing?" I asked when the truck slowed to a stop.

"Did you know a skunk was chasing you?" the driver said, laughing as he wiped his hand across the top of his mouth. They were large men, barely fitting the cab. I looked around for the gun.

"He wasn't chasing me," I snapped. "Did you shoot it?"

"Yeah, we killed it," the passenger said, speaking for the first time, his cap pulled low over his forehead.

The driver, though, knew I was angry and glanced over at his friend. "Nah," he said. "We just scared it away." He looked out the windshield. "Those people," he continued, and pointed to the two still-dark houses down the road. "If we hadn't've shot it, a car would have hit it, and then it would have smelled. Do you know how bad they smell?" He paused, his lips pressed into a grin or a grimace, and then finished, "We saved it from getting hit by a car."

By killing it, I thought. You saved it by killing it.

Cancer, Crohn's disease, diverticulitis, pancreatitis, perforations, super bacteria—these are the possibilities. If the blockage doesn't clear, they will cut him open. The NG tube continues to pump his stomach, collecting bile in a plastic container beneath his bed. The liquid comes from his nose and travels like a snake to the bottle. Slowly Michael's insides, fluids that are rarely seen, the body's secrets, make their way into daylight, yellowish-brown and sludgy.

The day passes quietly. We listen to classical music that I have brought from home, and I read *The Hobbit* out loud. The music keeps his mind off the NG tube, his sore throat and cracked lips, the fact that he must remain on his back. I have chosen music I know he likes but have left both Tchaikovsky and Beethoven at home, as these are the symphonies he wants to leave the world hearing. Whenever I listen to their notes, I think of the moment when Michael will no longer be at my side. For the hospital, I choose Erik Satie, Grieg, and Schumann. I choose Krishna Das. And this seems enough.

The doctors are pushing massive amounts of antibiotics into Michael, along with pain medication and fluids. Awake for longer stretches of time, he and I sit in the strips of weak sunshine that stream through the window and try not to think of going home. Good friends visit, but the interruptions are hard to take. We have made this small world, sharing the space on Michael's tiny bed, a world in which he and I bob along the surface of some unknown sea, serenaded by a single violin.

The naked man appeared one foggy morning in late October, before the sun had risen above the trees that eclipse Ann Arbor, the town where I was attending graduate school. I set out that morning to run under the streetlights, brown leaves crunching beneath my feet, the occasional car driving past. The morning was dark enough and I was deep enough into my run that at first I didn't see him. Several miles from my house, on a typically busy street near campus, he stepped out from the edge of my route, naked and masked and beating off. We were alone on the wet, empty streets. At my jump, my tiny cry, he laughed and followed me with his nakedness, brandishing his erect penis like a sword. I turned and sprinted all the way home.

Not until I had showered and walked to campus did I think to call the police. "Men like that are rarely violent," the female officer told me over the phone. "It's not worth the time to file a report." I sensed disapproval through the phone line and reassured her that I had the situation under control.

Rather than lose the routine of my running route, the hills and turns my feet knew by heart, I chose to believe the officer and kept to the same path. My heart raced, though, every time I passed the place where he had stood.

For months I did not see him, the winter too cold for nakedness. On days when I had to run the indoor track because of the weather, I missed the trident maples and the redbuds whose winter limbs calligraphied the skies, but I felt safer. Outside, I had taken to carrying my keys like tiny knives, switching them back and forth between my hands; their heft and my ability to outrun the world brought me comfort as I passed bushes, shadows, and side streets. With daylight savings, warmer weather, and the tulips, though, he appeared again, stepping out of the fog, closer this time and still naked, holding a red rag over his mouth to conceal his face. His eyes were dark, his body bare, and he got off when he saw my fear. He had been waiting for me all winter.

I ran directly to the police station. Barely able to catch my breath, I described the naked man in detail to the officer on duty. The evening shift is about to change, he told me, I had caught them at a bad time. If I waited for an hour or so, though, the incoming officer could drive me back to the place and see if he was still there. When I told him I thought I would instead go home, he assured me in parting that men like that are rarely violent. Walking home in the morning traffic, my sweat grew cold against my skin.

The third and final time the naked man appeared, he emerged from a hedge close enough to grab me. I screamed. Six feet tall and thick in the chest, he towered over me, his pale skin aflame under the streetlights. He still held the red rag, still held his penis, and met my eyes with his own, in no way tempted to look away. I froze in place, paralyzed by his physical presence, his size. His chest was bare and muscled, his hands, enormous. If he caught me, he would hurt me. I was no match for him.

Our tiny boat runs aground that night at 9 p.m. The vein holding the IV has collapsed; the fluid leaks into Michael's skin, causing his hand to swell. Several nurses try to find a new entrance, but dehydration has narrowed his veins. Seven times they skewer his body with a needle, prodding and exploring, only to fail. Michael is white.

After calling the doctor, they decide to put a PICC line in. I can tell by the way they reassure me, the fact that I have to sign a new waiver not holding them responsible for what happens, that this can't be good.

What they propose is pushing a wire-thin tube up his arm by way of an artery rather than a vein and then over his shoulder and down into his heart. At ten o'clock on the evening of our second day in the hospital, the eve of Thanksgiving, Michael's insides dripping like maple syrup into a plastic container, a tube down his throat that engages his gag reflex every so often, this wire-thin tube running through his artery to perch above his heart like a bird and create a passageway connecting the outside to the inside and allowing anything in the world to travel to the very organ that keeps him alive becomes our only option.

A whole team of nurses arrive and begin the preparations for minor surgery, draping Michael, the metal table, and anything close by in sterilized cloths. The nurses don green robes and masks. Michael's eyes are full of fear.

The nurse prepped for the procedure seems confident. In the way she arranges her tools, chooses her needle, and taps on his veins, she suggests that this is, indeed, no big deal. She is wrong. Michael's veins tighten in an effort to thwart the foreign object that attacks them. She sticks and sticks again. This after three nurses have already stuck him. This after hours without an IV or pain medicine. This after being told it would be nothing. The nurse keeps poking the wire against his collapsing artery, causing him to shriek in pain.

"Let's try an ultrasound," she says.

Relying on the interior image of his body, the map the ultrasound creates, doesn't help. We see only confirmation of failure, the artery's collapse; we no longer have to rely only on Michael's cries. I am transfixed by the black-and-white pictures on the tiny computer screen that reveal him from the inside out. Not four weeks ago we watched a similar monitor to see our baby bounce against my uterus, the rabbit heart given a form. But the inside of the body looks nothing like you expect. My uterus appeared webbed and barren, cold and windowless. My baby had no face. Michael's veins are not tunnels, throughways for blood and catheters and fluids that take away the pain. The inside of his body, like mine, is a cave murky and dark, a space void of angles, planes, and right corners I can measure. Here nothing resembles anything I have known.

A new nurse arrives, one who doesn't wash his hands even when Michael specifically asks him to. He wears no robe or mask, doesn't even appear to be a nurse, dressed in jeans and tennis shoes. This could be some stranger off the streets, I think, what can he possibly know of all that we can't see. It turns out, he is the Rambo of nurses. Scorning the ultrasound, the guide wire, all the tools the previous nurse insisted upon, he says he will "freehand it." And as if he himself were the one swimming up Michael's arteries, he threads the catheter up his arm and over the tricky part in his shoulder—the place where the artery divides and goes both to the head and to the heart—and leaves it resting right where it needs to be. At midnight, as we tip into Thanksgiving Day, the nurse starts the new fluids and Michael falls asleep.

Even though I live in the mountains, where trails abound for running, I prefer the roads. Most runners I know who live here don't understand my choice. The cars, they say, the ice, the pain of those hard surfaces. When I tell them that I run early and year-round, they usually nod their heads in understanding. If pressed, I will describe the repeatability of the road, the assurance asphalt gives and how I can then let my mind wander. But such certainty is a lie. Skunks and guns and naked men have all met me on the road. I have fallen many times, been chased by dogs, and become lost. I have also been forced to stop, not because of gunshot or injury, but because the clouds are lit from below by a dawn that only knows what it means to rise. In truth what I like about roads duplicates what I like about running itself, the illusion of control, even when I recognize that the unknown, the dark spaces, full of uncertainty and risk, give birth to the miracles. When King Arthur sends his knights in search of the Holy Grail, he exhorts them to travel alone and to enter the darkest parts of the forest and only where no paths exist. Anything precious, he suggests, can only be found where it is darkest.

Thanksgiving Day brings with it a miracle. Michael feels better. His eyes are less puffy, his skin less swollen, the color back. The blockage appears to be gone, surprising the doctor so much that he keeps running more tests to confirm this fact. We can, he thinks, go home on Saturday.

As quickly as the blockage appeared, it retreats, sinking back into Michael's body, dissolving into something else. Or at least so it seems. Technically, we learn the blockage didn't exist or at least wasn't the cause of his illness. The gastroenterologist we will see in a few days will describe how Michael's ileum, the final section of the small intestine, closed up. But he won't be able to say why. Michael tests negative for disease, for cancer. A microbe perhaps, but no one knows for sure. For the next several years, every time Michael has a stomachache, he will think his insides are collapsing again.

That day in the hospital we make plans, lying together on the bed. We close our eyes, ignore the pinging of the intercom, the machines clicking and whirring, the shuffle of feet outside our door, and I describe the beautiful places we have been: the Nā Pali coast, Glacier, Yellowstone, the beaches in Sicily, the hills around our house and the way they erupt in patches of raucous sunflowers in June. Michael answers me now and then, adds a detail, reminds me of something I have forgotten. I am grateful for all that he offers.

Sitting on the hospital bed next to Michael, warm with color, I do not tell him of the landscape inside his own body, the thicket of veins that run in and out of one another, webbed tissue, like winter tree limbs, cathedraling at the edges. I do not tell him about collapsing arteries, his insides tensing with every jab, or how the caverns of his body reminded me of our unborn child. I do not share the knowledge that our first landscape, the one we have long forgotten, the first body that housed our own, stretches vast and unknown. To have forgotten the mystery of that initial landscape—the folds and curves, the rivers and caves—seems the most damaging of losses to me that day; to try to name it, harness it, control it, the greatest of follies.

Our son, Aidan, will be born four months and a day after we leave the hospital. A doctor will pull him from my body with a plunger because I will be unwilling to offer him to this world. Before Michael's illness, I would have explained the long labor and ultimate assistance by suggesting I wanted to keep him inside of me where he was safe. I valued what could be controlled and controlled all that I could. On the night of delivery, the doctor brandishing the vacuum, perhaps my body chose to keep my son inside, to allow him to linger as long as possible in a place of creeks and caverns, not because it was safe but because it would never be recalled.

Within five weeks, I will be running again, slowly at first, both skin and muscles tight. In my strides, short and heavy, I no longer recognize myself. In this new body, this mother's body, strength is not so clearly defined. Above, the dark dome of the early morning sky stretches its embrace over the valley, and I hear the first meadowlark of the spring. I round the final corner of the country road, grateful to have the wind at my back.

The Cemetery

A cemetery sits at the center of my life. Actually, it sits at the end of a dirt road about a mile from my house, but it might as well be the very place my blood pools and gathers before wending its way back through my body. In the past two years I have walked to the cemetery every day, many times twice a day, often with Michael, sometimes alone, or with our dog, more recently with Aidan, a blanket draped over the stroller to shade him. I realized the other day that in the past two years I have probably made the cemetery walk six hundred times, close to the same number of times I have laid my head on my pillow to sleep, eaten breakfast, or put on my underwear. I could walk other places—up the road to visit the neighbor's goat or across the street to check on the dairy farm—but I don't. Every day I turn right when coming out of the driveway and wander down to the dirt road. Somehow the idea that a cemetery rests at the center of my life doesn't feel strange. Or perhaps the cemetery centers me, something to do with its windfall of trees amid this high desert plateau, or maybe it has to do with walking.

Whitney Cemetery is a relatively young cemetery. In the West, non-Natives have only been burying their dead for the past hundred and fifty years or so. Friends from the East who come to visit describe cemeteries in Boston or Connecticut that have headstones dating back to the colonies. I imagine their marble surfaces have worn smooth through centuries of weather and neglect, dissolving the names of the dead, monument following corpse back into the earth. Here, though, in my cemetery, you rarely see a headstone from before the late 1800s, and even those are infrequent. Whitney and the surrounding area were first settled by non-Natives in the 1860s. While I am sure people began dying immediately, establishing a collective place to bury them likely took some time. You need to believe you will remain in a place before consigning your dead to the earth in any organized way.

Whitney is also a Mormon cemetery, as it was the Latter-day Saints who established towns in this part of Idaho. One of a number of small cemeteries in the area, all of which are marked by a grove of trees, the Whitney Cemetery erupts vertically from an otherwise relatively treeless valley floor. So when I say it is my cemetery, I am using the possessive in the loosest of ways. None of my relatives are buried here; none of the names on the headstones appear in the narrative I tell of my past. I am an outsider to the Mormon belief system and a stranger in this tiny town. Nevertheless, Michael and I are the only people who visit these dead daily, and while we never bring flowers or tend the gravesites, such use seems to bring with it a measure of responsibility, if not possession.

I have met the actual caretaker, Dave Weaver, a worn man who smiles freely and is always willing to stop his work and chat. He lives up the street from us in a house fronted by so many aspens that in the summer you cannot see his door. Years of work in the cemetery must have made him crave the companionship of trees, and now he both works and sleeps amid the rustling of leaves. Dave is a fourth-generation sexton. He inherited his trade from his father, the occupation of gravedigger handed down like a recipe or antique chest of drawers. Because, while he spends his days cutting the grass and making sure the sprinklers are working, his main job, the real work, is digging. Dave's father dug 350 graves in his lifetime before bequeathing the job to his son.

Today, in other towns, most graves are dug by backhoe, but here in Whitney, Idaho, a rural town where the old are growing older and the young are moving away, the graves are dug with a shovel, and the entire process takes about two days.

Grave digging is a craft, akin to leatherwork or blacksmithing. You only have to see one of Dave's graves to realize how much will be lost if the tradition is not passed down. With perfectly pitched sides, not a root or rock to disrupt the cool, black surface, Dave's graves are beautiful, inviting. I want to jump into them, lie down, take the dirt he has carefully placed to the side and pull it over me like a quilt. That something in the natural world can be so perfectly squared, tidy, and neat is a tiny miracle. Standing over the grave, late in the day when the crickets are beginning to chirr and hum and the cool from the recently dug hole wraps my ankles like a vine, I see his work as a gift, the last gift, given to the dead, a womb of earth, a bed.

I have seen Dave dig about a half dozen graves. Often we come upon him in the afternoon, his head barely above the earth, piles of dirt to both sides growing steadily as he removes the four tons necessary for a standard grave. Our dog barks—after all men are usually above the ground and not in it—but the barking doesn't seem to bother Dave. He waves cheerfully, and we all pretend that his shoveling does not mean one more person has just left a life that he or she loved fully and completely. Sometime later he must use a tool to smooth the sides like fondant on a cake. Because by the next day, the grave stands clean and ready, and the day after that it is covered with wreaths and flowers and a strip of AstroTurf that conceals the scar in the earth until the grass can grow again.

All this makes it sound as though the cemetery is a depressing place. After all, besides the sexton and the county clerk, Michael and I are probably the only ones who keep abreast of the death rate in Whitney. And such knowledge should feel heavy. But

Dave literally whistles while he works, and I feel only gratitude for such lovely graves. Perhaps I would feel differently if the dead were my own. Perhaps I would feel differently if I had lived for generations on this land. But mostly I cannot wait to reach the cemetery, to move from the open dirt road surrounded by alfalfa fields and merge into the shadows of the trees. Mostly I feel alive amid all that death, thankful for the many shades of green and the sound leaves make in the wind.

When Aidan was only a week old, Michael and I took him to the cemetery on his first outing. I had to walk slowly, my body still sore and stitched from birth, each step reminding me that Aidan had come into this greening world out of me. Our dog, Pippin, walked with us, assuming the position alongside the stroller that he would maintain for the next many months. It was the second week of April, and spring had exploded in the forty-eight hours we had been in the hospital. The Bradford pears lining the driveway to the emergency room had, days before, been filled only with buds, but they wagged heavy white blossoms as we left. The trees in the cemetery—maples, crab apples, cottonwoods, oak, and ash—were just beginning to leaf out, throwing dots of bright green against winter-bare limbs. We showed Aidan the hawks and the sweet blue flowers, we let him feel the wind moving over the fields, and we welcomed him into the natural world amid hundreds of graves.

He knows the cemetery as well as he knows his own bed. Often in the afternoons, I take him up there, and we lie amid the graves and watch the leaves dance against the sky. He loves the movement and remains content for a long time. Lately he has taken to pulling up the grass that grows over the graves, catching four or five spears and bringing them to his mouth for a taste. For him, the cemetery is a place of life, a green and growing place.

Sometimes I wonder what others might think, people whose relatives are buried there, people whose names are already inscribed on headstones, awaiting only their death for completion. I wonder what they would think if they saw me nursing Aidan as I sit on a bench not four feet away from the gravesite of a church prophet, or if they saw Pippin running with abandon, or if they watched me push the stroller over graves to reach a place in the shade where we can enjoy the antics of the hawks. On the rare occasions when someone comes up to the cemetery while we are there, I generally try to corral the dog and stay on the gravel road. I imagine they would not like the way I use the place, would call my casual wanderings inappropriate or disrespectful. But it is not that I do not find the place sacred, for I do. Rather, for me, every place is sacred and worthy of being beheld. Why only honor particular patches of land and the dead who can be named? Every spear of grass that Aidan will ever pull from the earth covers someone's body. The cemetery resembles the backyard or the surrounding fields.

And yet.

According to the map that stands in the middle of the cemetery, Marie Benson was the first person buried there, in May of 1890. She was five years old. The newly planted cottonwoods that stand along the east edge of the cemetery would have just begun snowing down their cottonseeds, stirring in the mourners recent memories of a harsh winter and wicked wind. The cottonwoods, now more than a hundred years old, rise like skyscrapers against the Idaho sky. They are home to red-tailed hawks and great horned owls, giant birds that swoop when we approach, shriek their annoyance, and circle off into the fields to await our passage. In 1890, though, I imagine Marie's family huddled together on the bluff overlooking Spring Creek, few trees to block the wind as it swept down from Red Rock Pass, committing their tiny daughter's body to an empty stretch of ground. Perhaps they found themselves hoping that more bodies would follow so they did not have to leave Marie alone. Perhaps they knew on that raw spring day in a new land that Marie was only the first of many.

She was. Sidney Gilbert followed a few months later. Born in 1890. Died the same year. On his grave marker, a tired marble slab, all that can be read are his name and the date. Unlike Marie, whose body was tucked away in what has become the southeast corner of the cemetery, Sidney was buried in the middle. A beautiful blue spruce rises near his headstone, and I wonder if it was planted the same year he died. The spruce trees around our house are a hundred years old, planted the year our house was built, a decade after Sidney's death. They tower over the house, throwing an afternoon shadow that runs across the street and rises up the hill on our neighbor's property. Buttressed on all sides by these giants, we have always felt our home was a nest. During the frequent windstorms it can feel as though we too are swaying, caught in their boughs, gently swinging. If I were Sidney's mother, I would have insisted that a spruce be planted by my infant son's grave, a grave that sat alone, atop a gentle rise, a mile from town. Perhaps, I would have hoped, the tree might sing my baby to sleep when I no longer could.

But I am not Sidney's mother, I am Aidan's, and learning that my cemetery initially held the bodies of babies and children rather than those of the elderly, after fully lived lives, sobers me. I would imagine, here, what burying your child is really like, but I cannot. Not even for the sake of story.

More babies are buried. Many, many, many more. The headstone that moves me the most, the one I always point visitors to, and the one I always visit in my mind even when I don't visit on foot, is for the Newbold family. A testament to loss. Reo Newbold, born in 1912, married Margaret. She was two years his senior, scandalous maybe, but I imagine they were in love. Likely they married during the Great Depression when there was very little hope. Maybe they had moved out here from back east, hoping that dairy cows or sugar beets would provide a family income. Maybe Reo had a brother who had moved first and sent letters home that described a valley cut by the Bear River, fertile and empty, urging Reo to leave his job at the steel factory and take a chance. Maybe it was Margaret who, tired of long hours and double shifts, late at night when they were both in bed, whispered of a better life, a new start. For whatever reason, they found themselves in Whitney, Idaho, teetering on the edge of Zion, the Mormon promised land.

Baby Boy Newbold lies buried with Margaret. No date for his death etched on the stone, but the writer in me imagines that his mother died in childbirth, after years of trying to conceive, leaving Reo alone with his dairy cows, the promise sullied, the land not easy or forgiving.

Or not. Reo is also married to Blanche, ten years his junior. Whether at the same time he is married to Margaret remains unclear. Marriage dates are left off the headstone, but all are buried together; a man, his wives, and his children sealed in eternity. My guess is that Reo had two wives. Even though at the time polygamy was outlawed, it was not uncommon. The house we own, one built by the grandfather of a church prophet, has a second house not twenty yards from the main house, the perfect place to keep a second family. From the upstairs window where Michael has his study, I imagine the first wife keeping tabs on the second, wondering to herself as she absently wipes dust from the window sill which bed her husband will choose that evening. She stands eight months pregnant, her belly thrust out like the prow of a ship, making it all the more likely he will choose her sister wife, a woman twelve years her junior. The sister wife's house is not as grand as her own, she tells herself by way of comfort. A simple staircase leads to the second floor, nothing like her stunning hand-carved banister that runs the length of her own. He may choose her bed, she thinks, but I am the one with the twin parlors. Drawing her fingers along the wood molding that surrounds the window, she thinks the parlors enough.

But I am imaging the woman who lived in our house, and that is not Blanche. Blanche lives with Margaret and Reo on the dairy farm. And unlike Margaret, who has had trouble getting pregnant, Blanche finds that her body is made for carrying babies. When Margaret dies in 1940, Blanche is just beginning what will become two decades of birthing. By the time she dies in 1995, Blanche will have given birth fourteen times. For close to fourteen years she will fall asleep to the pulse of a double heartbeat. Fourteen times she will catch her breath when her baby first begins to move. More than a hundred months will be spent wondering, awaiting a new, tiny being.

Only half of her babies, though, will live longer than a day. Seven die. While carrying babies presents no problem, keeping them alive does. Next to Blanche and Margaret and Reo's grave runs a low, thin headstone marking the place where seven babies are buried. Every infant died the day it was born, with the exception of one who lived to a second, a spring day I find myself hoping. To consign one child to the grave seems impossible to me. Seven, incomprehensible.

Reo and Blanche name them all, and all fourteen names, the living and the dead, are engraved on their headstone along with Margaret and Baby Boy. I know enough of Mormon theology to understand the importance of listing the fruit of their union. As a Mormon male, a priest imbued with godlike abilities, Reo will ascend to higher levels of heaven the more children he has. His offspring are sealed to him in the temple, bonded to him for eternity. While Blanche will have to wait and see if Reo calls to her from the other side, inviting her into heaven, Reo's place in the eternal kingdom is assured because his wives have borne him fifteen children. In the past, I have always felt a mix of sympathy and anger toward Blanche. She was pregnant for close to a fourth of her life, and babies nursed at her breast for half of her days. More painfully, she saw seven babies laid in the ground. I imagine her sitting with each newborn in her hands, the pain of labor endured so often that it has become a companion, waiting to see if this one will live through the night. Can she endure another loss? Can she let another go? Outside the bedroom door, her other children clamor for her attention, wanting, wanting, wanting. She looks down at the tiny bundle in her arms and notes his ragged breathing. Moments ago his skin was rosy pink and now it has taken on a sallow color, like the belly of a maple leaf in the fall. The neighbor women have left, leaving Reo alone with his wife. Noting the baby's difficulties, he sighs aloud and rises, gathering his hat along with the forgotten bloody sheets and candle stubs. Turning from Blanche's bedside, he finds himself wondering whether the ground has frozen yet.

Reo. Reo. For two years now my sympathies have been with Blanche, whose body was bent from birthing. But now I think of Reo, imagine him as he buries yet another child, throwing a handful of dirt over the grave, trying not to notice that the grave has been dug too close to the others and that the wooden edge of a rotting casket can been seen, worrying his hands along his thighs because they will not remain in his pockets, and wondering when all this dying will end.

Cemetery, from the Greek for burial place and the Latin for cradle. Death and birth linked at the level of language, a connection I reaffirm each day when I am making the rounds of the dead with my infant son. Standing at the Newbold grave, brushing leaves away with my foot so that I can see the engraved names that muster like soldiers, I look to Aidan who has fallen asleep in the stroller, watch his chest rising, and pull the blanket up around him.

Aidan's birth on a day in April brought more than the blossoming of Bradford pears. With his arrival came the attendant possibility of unbearable loss, a presence that catches like a cloud on a mountain, keeping the valley in shadow. Walking in the cemetery as light splashes through autumn maples to land on the ground in galloping rivers of color, I am struck by the testimony given by land and marble. There is so much green, so much brightness, so much life in this tiny plot of land, but tangled up with the leaves and the hawks and the blades of grass that can live as long as trees is a record of personal devastation. Standing at its center, the ash tree fountaining into the sky, I imagine the lives of Blanche and Reo, whose decisions ribbon across generations and wonder to myself if Dave's back hurts at night. The Newbold graves now free of leaves and Aidan still asleep, I commit my feet in the direction of home, knowing that with my departure the hawks return to their nests.

Openings

You cannot open the pickles, so you ask your father, who is visiting for the holidays and hunched at the dining room table playing solitaire. Only moments before he announced that he had accomplished the impossible by winning back-to-back hands, the sound of triumph in his voice wafting into the kitchen like a forgotten smell.

"My thumbs," he mutters, staring at his hands as if he does not recognize them. And then he tries to open the jar.

As a child, in church, while the priest droned on about Peter and Paul and the children in front of you drove dented cars along the kelp-green kneelers, you held your father's hands, rubbed the wire-thin scabs left by errant two-by-fours or nails that popped when hammered askew, and wound your own slender fingers in between his, measuring their girth. He had his mother's hands, and with them he could move logs in the fireplace without tongs, take casseroles from the oven without mitts, brand the back of your legs with a swat. Covered with freckles and marbled by dryness, his hands could hold you hard to the floor as you fought to flee his tickling. Small hands for such a large man, he always said. Large hands to such a small girl.

The jar won't open even after he bangs the top against the tiled floor. When he moves to the kitchen for a hammer and screwdriver, you head in the other direction, toward your bedroom, imagining the shattered glass and the visit to the emergency room, unwilling to witness the quiet desperation with which he confronts the jar, shutting the door behind you.

Days later, he will carry your second son, Kellen, born two years after Aidan, into the desert, hold the tiny body against his stomach, watch his feet along the trail, the cactus, the pebbles that threaten to roll beneath his feet. Every five minutes, you will offer to take your son, remember the pickles, the thumbs, the way his eyes flickered at the prospect of failure, but he declines. Maybe he too recalls the moment, the way you left the room. Rattlesnake Trail refuses to end, the pitch of the land becoming steeper, the saguaro, taller. When he finally relinquishes your son, both their foreheads are slick with sweat; he will have carried him for miles.

When you return from the bedroom, the jar is sitting on the kitchen counter, the pickles bobbing in the briny water, the yellow lid resting to the side.

Sometimes you think you notice a trace of the Parkinson's that took your uncle in your father's hands, a tremor, a tremble, a casual shaking. The more your look for it, the more you notice the way your father hides his hands, buries them in pockets, keeps them fisted. He spread the same chemicals over the acres of farmland, handled the same poisons, breathed the same fertilizers as his older brother. The legacy of nerve damage cuts as true a line as any Nebraska country road.

"Thanks for the pickles," you call to your father, who has resumed his card game in hopes of winning a third before the evening ends. "Your mother opened it," he says, the cards pausing for a second, perhaps the eight of clubs not yet played, winning still possible, while you stand in the kitchen, out of his sight, holding the open jar in your hands.

Running through the Dark

This morning while I was running, shoes smacking the pavement, Venus bright above the spine of the Bear Mountains, and my thoughts pinned to the day ahead, the meetings, the deadlines, the writing I would not do, a deer was hit by a car. It flew in front of me, disrupting the morning stillness, veered close to my chest, and then into the oncoming lane; for a moment, its legs silhouetted against the headlights of the SUV like a shadow puppet. Perhaps a mother scurrying after her baby, who had already crossed the street. Perhaps the baby chasing its mother's tail, too young to know of cars or roads or the way high beams devour your ability to see in shadow.

"Is the deer okay?" the woman asks, stepping from her car, the interior lit by the opening of her door, bright and warm in shades of beige, the silver glint of a coffee mug like a lantern on the dash.

"I don't know," I respond, my mittens still over my mouth. And I move from worrying about the deer to worrying about this stranger in the dark, bundled in a red jacket that she zips securely under her chin. "You barely hit his legs," I say, consciously choosing the gender, thinking the loss of him is somehow less than the loss of her on this still-dark morning.

"Are you okay?"

"Yes," she says. "I'm sorry."

"It's okay," I reassure her. "They always run across the road."

And I turn from the brush on the side of the road to resume my run.

A crack, I think, as I move down the hill, the sound of bone breaking, delicate but decided. She is not okay. Fled to the brush but not to safety. She will die, maybe not today but within weeks, unable to graze the valley floor or shot by a hunter during the season that opens in a week. A crack is what I remember now more than the legs held in amber. The pounding of my feet, always a flat runner, never with the kick of a marathoner, never light and nimble, suggests with every stride that I caused the deer to scurry from the brush and into the road.

"I'm sorry," she says to me, the only witness in the dark, and I forgive her because no other options exist. They always run across the road.

She doesn't know I am to blame.

This morning I hit a deer while running. Most likely she is dead. By the bottom of the hill, I have opened Toni Morrison's "menu of regret." My failures spill freely onto the pavement, the accident having driven a wedge into the room of my heart that I try to keep locked. "People don't like mean boys," I say to Aidan. "No one will play with you." And when Kellen butts his toddler head into mine because he wants another story, instead of opening *Goodnight Moon* again, I dump him roughly into his crib. My friend has no children, has no job, writes all day in her windowed house high in the mountains, while I steal two hours at a noisy bookstore before I head to campus and cut corners on my teaching, send apologies over email like Valentines. When I was seven I hurt my father. At thirty-seven I did the same. I steep anger into my husband's morning tea.

Orion fades above me in the bowl of sky, while dawn simmers at the ridgeline, black to blue, providing only enough light to reveal the school children huddled together for the bus. Where is the deer now? Lying down beneath the stars, licking a wound that she cannot heal? How will I protect my sons from this world, from the way it insists on suffering, from a mother who used to do everything well and now limps through the day?

Out in the West

"I try to focus on the positive," David tells me. His body leans forward in the chair as if his thin frame will add heft to a statement that his eyes don't support. "I'm fine."

Sitting with my college students in my office, I often try to picture Aidan and Kellen in their teens. Right now any despair in the house arrives from the necessity of sharing toys, not secrets. But there will come a day, I know, when they, like David, will need help, and I will no longer be there. My hope for them will be an office on a second floor and someone willing to listen.

Outside the windows, the campus sits brown and empty. Late fall is the only time of the year when northern Utah loses its beauty, a girl without her party dress. Snow has not yet covered the mountains that rise all around us. Bereft of leaves and birds, they seem to huddle closer to the ground. The semester has hit the same brown patch as the season, far from the beginning but not close enough to the end to count. The radiator bangs to life, pinging like a mechanical heart.

"I know of someone you can talk to," I say. "Her voice mail is password protected. Any message you left would be safe."

"Thanks," he says, "but I'm fine."

I return to his essay, the sheaf of paper bending in my hand, and read my marginal comments. In pencil I have asked him to "flesh things out" or "set the scene." These questions of craft feel like another shore at this moment, an island distant and foreign.

What I want to do is shake him, beg him to leave the valley, head for the coast. What I want to do is hold him in my arms and tell him that everything will be okay. But I don't. We sit in silence, the radiator's last beat echoing down the hall.

"You're so hard on yourself in your essay. I'm worried about you."

He laughs nervously and shakes his head, then wipes his hands up and down his jeans to scrub a stain no one can see.

I can't tell him I am worried he will kill himself. I have said as much to other students, but I knew them better. David is buried in his down-filled coat, far away from me. I think about giving him the statistics for gay teen suicide, pointing out the fact that Utah's numbers are higher than the national average, but figures wouldn't matter in this conversation.

"Okay," I say and push my rolling office chair toward the bookcase, wishing I could keep on pushing it, out the window, into the sky, and then up over these mountains with their thousand-year-old juniper hunkering into barren north faces, to a place with more color, more moisture, more oxygen, a place where I could fill my lungs with more air and less God.

Before leaving my office, David will take the piece of paper with the phone number on it. I will watch him shove the folded note into his backpack with his books, a laptop, and several worn spiral notebooks. I imagine it remains there.

I am in the grocery store, standing in line waiting to check out. A voice overhead announces a special on ground beef, while the child in front of me begs his mother for a candy bar, collapsing into a pile of tears when she denies him. As I often do, I scan the headlines of the magazines to keep abreast of the beautiful people's latest misfortunes. I tell myself, when I reach for *People* and add it to my cart, that I must keep current for my students, that I am a better teacher because I know the most recent episode in the life of Lindsay Lohan. I resist flipping through the "Star Tracks" until I arrive home.

The magazine rack holds the titles you would expect: the *National Enquirer, Good Housekeeping, Vogue,* etc., though many of the covers are concealed behind brown squares of plastic. Instead of seeing the cover of *Vogue,* I read the title in white vinyl letters across the plastic sheet. *Good Housekeeping* sits plainly visible, as does *Family Day.* The magazines that are concealed are those that reveal women and their skin.

Just how much skin matters is a calculus I have tried to work out in the past ten years I have lived here. With every visit to the grocery store, I conduct an informal survey to see if I can determine how much becomes too much for this predominately Mormon state. What I have learned is that bare shoulders and midriffs are unacceptable, but arms are okay. Legs must be covered from the knees up. The person in front of me finishes, and my groceries move forward on the belt. As I have done many times before, I remove the plastic shields from every magazine in checkout line number nine, leaving a quivering sea of flesh behind me.

David's essay begins when, at the age of fifteen, he is mowing the lawn one afternoon. As his father's car makes its way up the driveway, David can smell the stench long before the car stops in front of him. His father tells him that the kittens David has been nursing the past few weeks have climbed up into the engine of the car and died there. David must scrape them out. What follows is one of the cruelest scenes I have read in ten years of students writing memoir for me. David slides under the car, face only inches from the engine, and pulls bits of kitten from the metal, the flesh popping with the release of pressure, maggots falling to the ground. At one point, he scrambles out, gasping for breath, begging his father to take the task from him, only to return to what he describes as a second world, a darker one, one full of stain, stench, and displeasure. In the end, he stands before his father bloodied and undone. The shine from his father's white shirt almost blinds him after his time under the engine.

In the next scene, David reveals he is gay and Mormon.

Utah is eighty-five percent Mormon, but you can't understand the length of Zion's reach until you live here. I will always be an outsider. After a decade, though, I have made a kind of peace with the state. You have to if you want to remain. The peace is hard-earned, uneasy, and tested continually. And it has been the Church of Jesus Christ of Latter-day Saints' stance on homosexuality that has most recently challenged any goodwill I have fostered over the years and makes me question the decision to raise our boys here.

In official documents, the church takes pains to describe the place of their gay members. They don't deny that same-sex "inclination" might exist, though they are quick to point out that "gratefully . . . same-gender attraction did not exist in the pre-earth life and neither will it exist in the next life." Past president Gordon Hinkley, once the prophet for the church, the one who speaks for God, has said that gay Mormons can obtain every other reward promised to all good Mormons as long as they don't act on their homosexuality. Gays and lesbians are free to remain in the church, serve a mission, and conduct temple work as long as they "control" their "inclination."

More recently, Boyd K. Packer, an LDS apostle privy to the voice of God, told millions of his followers that same-sex attraction is "impure and unnatural." His speech came a week following a string of gay teen suicides across the country. But Packer assures his followers that same-sex attraction represents no more temptation than alcohol or anger. If you have the inclination for drink or sex, then God has given you the attendant means to control it. If you fail to do so, the weakness resides in you.

Michael and I had only lived in Zion for a few weeks when Ezekiel paid us his first visit. Close to ninety and crippled by arthritis, Ezekiel was our neighbor to the south. Walking the stretch of lawn between our houses took him close to half an hour, each step slow and calculated, a long pause in between, the length of a prayer. When he got to the concrete steps of our porch, he would fall to his knees, where he had carefully strapped on his gardening pads. Then he would climb our stairs on his hands and knees, pull himself up by the doorknob, and ring our bell. Upon learning we were nonbelievers, he undertook our salvation, arriving monthly, often bearing fruit from his garden as a gift, along with his testimony.

We tolerated his visits because we had just moved to the neighborhood and didn't want to offend. But his persistence became annoying. "If you read the Book of Mormon with an open heart," he would say, "then you will know it is true." Some days he would describe how often he prayed for us. Other days, the temple work his wife was doing in our name. Pamphlets were wedged in our door, paperback copies of Mormon literature left on our steps. Michael and I would find ourselves hiding in our own house, asking, "Do you think he's still there?" I threw the zucchini away, along with the books. I felt that accepting anything from him meant accepting all of it.

Perhaps it was the same spring a student called me a "feminazi" on my teaching evaluations; perhaps it was the day after I had been told only my husband's name could appear on the phone bill; or maybe it was the morning I overheard the manager tell a racist joke in the local NAPA auto parts store and had done nothing about it. From the kitchen window, I saw Ezekiel walking toward our house, his hands empty this time. Instead of hiding in the upstairs study, I opened the door before he could even ring, just as he picked up his body from the ground. "Come in."

Even though the early spring weather was cool, a line of sweat stood out on his forehead, unconcealed by the few strands of thin, gray hair. He chased after his breath, held his bent and crooked arms to his chest. In such a state, he still managed a smile. "Yes, thank you," he said.

Once inside the house, I helped him up the stairs to the living room. I could feel the thin bones in his arms, the push of his ribs. He was a sack of a man. At any other moment, such fragility in a human being would have cast me back on my own mortality. Now, his efforts just incensed me.

He collapsed into the couch, back rounded like a child's, his breath still coming quickly. I offered him water, the only beverage in the house I knew he could drink. As I filled his glass in the kitchen, I imagined him looking around the room at the figures of Buddha and Shiva on the bookshelf, the temple rubbings from Thailand, the Sanskrit wall hangings. We had no picture of Joseph Smith, no set of wooden blocks spelling out "Family" or "Love," no American flags. We had no television. Any direction he looked would have unsettled him. When I returned to the living room, he gazed steadily at his shoes.

"Have you read the books I have given you?" he asked, taking the glass from me. I noticed his hand shook, the water sloshing at the rim. "Have you prayed on them?"

Even though I had been the one to invite him in, I realized I wanted him gone. Perhaps by opening the door, I had given something away.

Standing in front of his broken form, my urge was to undress, to throw my clothes off and stand naked in front of him, feel the weak sun shining through the picture window on my bare skin. I wanted to be seen. I wanted him to take notice of who I was, not someone to convert but someone who could refuse his version of salvation and still not be lost.

He continued to talk about scripture, about God's plan, a speech he knew by heart and delivered without pause. I stood before him. I brought my hands to the hem of my T-shirt, felt the raw edge of the fabric, lifted the hem. The early spring air sent shivers up my arms as it found my bare skin. He continued, as if I weren't even in the room. I imagined my nakedness blinding him, imagined him shielding his gaze from my breasts.

Then I looked closer at his eyes, rheumy and white. I realized that arthritis alone wasn't responsible for his agonizing journey to our house. I would never be seen.

Clothed and standing, I screamed, "We don't want to become Mormon!" He flinched, drew his hand to his chest, and was silent.

Several weeks after I banished Ezekiel from our house, weeks in which we no longer drank wine on our deck and drew our blinds when the late afternoon sun still hung in the sky, Michael returned from a weekend trip. It was the first time I had been left alone in Zion. Each night he was gone, I locked the doors and took a plumber's wrench to bed. At the time, I think I would have said I was scared of wild animals, an errant bear, a coyote on the prowl. While we did indeed live in a rural community in the foothills of the Intermountain West, a rogue bear would have been an irrational fear. Lightning was a much more reasonable danger. Only now do I recognize the fear for what it was, the vague feeling I carried with me every morning as I shut the door to our house behind me and stepped into the daylight: that I was unwanted in this community, that my presence was a threat to those around me.

Such a fear wouldn't have been unfounded. In those early years, Michael and I took turns writing letters to the editor complaining about what we saw as the ignorance around us, the gender bias in the local newspaper, the unchallenged homophobia, the disapproval of drinking, sex before marriage, bare shoulders, anything that wasn't sanctioned by the church. Several times, others responded directly in the newspaper with letters of their own telling us that if we didn't like it here we should leave. This is who we are, the letters seemed to say. Be like us or be gone.

The morning of Michael's return, I watched for his red pickup truck from the window. When it came into sight on the long country road, I ran outside to meet him. Before Michael had even set his bags down, I said, "Guess what was in our yard!"

He paused and looked at me, considering the question. The truck's engine ticked quietly in the driveway. I imagine he could feel the urgency of my question, after all I hadn't even said hello to him. He had driven six hours to make it back home, likely had to pee, wanted to stretch his legs, take a warm bath. Instead he was confronted by my presence in the driveway, arms gesticulating wildly.

"A burning cross?"

I followed his gaze to the front yard, expecting to see the burned patch in our lawn, the smell of charred grass hovering in the air. At that moment, we thought such a thing was possible, that we could be hated that much.

"No," I said. "A moose. I saw a moose."

Like many Christians, Mormons have a strong belief in eternity. The next life drives this life, their time on the planet a "mortal probation." The belief in the next life doesn't just shape the actions in this life; it almost negates this life all together. When a Mormon man and woman are married in the temple, they are "sealed" to one another for "time and all eternity." Their children are "sealed" to them as well, so they enter their marriage believing that their family will be together forever.

For them, evidence of the world's corruption exists all around us, in those magazine covers, in R-rated movies, in men having sex with other men. But in the celestial kingdom all will be restored. So, for example, if your child has Down syndrome in this life, then in the celestial kingdom her body will be made whole. If your child is gay, as long as he never acts on his homosexuality and remains a member in good standing, in the celestial kingdom he will marry a woman and populate the world with spirit children.

When you are twenty and Mormon, eternity has a fairly strong pull on you, especially if all of your family will be hanging out in the celestial kingdom for time and all eternity. The promise of a whole body is compelling when you are taught your own body is impure. Years ago, a female student of mine, a closeted lesbian, said she would rather cut off her arm than leave the church. She prayed daily to God to make her straight. This fall I received a wedding announcement from her. She is marrying a man. They will be married in the temple.

A month ago, I was walking on campus with Aidan, now five. Michael and I constantly weigh the pros and cons of living where we live: a beautiful town nestled in a valley where classical music plays on NPR when the rest of the country is listening to the traffic report, but also a town on the northernmost edge of a state that supports ideas, laws, and beliefs we find untenable. Like many of our friends, we worry. There are no answers, but there are almost daily experiences that renew the conversation. That afternoon, Aidan and I were on our way to swimming lessons, and the bag full of towels and dry clothes pulled against my shoulder. Daylight savings time had just ended, so the evening felt especially dark even though it wasn't yet five o'clock. It was a warm fall evening, and the chickadees gathered in the limbs above us, enjoying the space left after most of the other birds had headed south.

We walked along the main street through campus. Student groups had recently painted brightly colored murals on the asphalt as part of Homecoming activities. The colors remained vivid even a month later and seemed to glow in the dark. Last year, the mural painted by the Gay Lesbian Bisexual Transgender Center was defaced, a bucket of black paint smeared over rainbow figures holding hands. What had taken students an entire night to create was destroyed in minutes. Many on campus saw the act as a hate crime, though Utah has no hate crime legislation.

This year the rainbow-colored figures remained, buttressed on either side by the murals painted by food service workers and student athletes. Each week Aidan asked about the pictures as we walked by, waited for the moment we approached the one with the Aggie Bull. I always made sure to point to the picture of the rainbowed children, reminding him that anyone can love anyone in this world.

Near the crosswalk at the heart of campus, a pickup truck roared past, silencing the chickadees and causing Aidan to flinch. We stepped farther away from the street as the black truck blazed by us. A confederate flag waved above the window where two men hung out screaming "Fag, fag, fag."

"What are they saying, Mommy?" Aidan asked.

Such a simple question. Such an impossible answer. My first thought was to drop to my knees and try to explain to my kindergartner how fear makes us full of hate. But then I looked to the right. A student who stood near us unlocking his bike met my eyes. He was wearing pastel madras pants. We were the only three people on the street. I wanted to tell the student to head for the library, for a lighted building, for a crowd. I wondered if he knew that Logan's designation as one of the safest cities in the United States depends entirely on who you are.

David has made the choice, for now, to stay in the church and focus on other things in his life. When he told his father he was gay, his father stayed on script and told him he loved him no matter what before describing how the church could keep him strong. They sat in their truck in the church parking lot, a streetlight illuminating their hands. Then his father described his own addiction to porn. Utah has the highest internet pornography rate in the country, another product of the fierce sexual repression. The struggle is almost a cliché around here. Without the church, David's father says he would not have been able to fight his ongoing addiction. Two men, sitting in a parking lot, a street light encircling the cab of their truck.

David ends his essay by looking out over the lights of the city and noticing a sickly yellow light amid all the white ones. He is, he says, that sickly yellow light, the one stained, the one in hell under the car, maggots falling all around him. He can no longer breathe.

My reassurance that his sexuality is both natural and acceptable cannot change the fact that when he sits in church he hears that his feelings are immoral. He will be redeemed, he is told, he will be made whole. He only has to sacrifice this one life.

The first time missionaries came to our door, we had moved to the house near the cemetery, the one that sat directly across from the LDS church. The local bishop had visited to tell us that our not being married would lead to certain ruin, but for the most part we had been left alone once word got around that we were nonbelievers. Which is why I was so surprised when I opened the door that afternoon and saw two missionaries in front of me.

"Hello," they said in unison, grinning with the sun. "I'm Elder Beck and this is Elder Smith. What's your name?"

"I'm not becoming Mormon," I said.

I had been baking, and flour dusted the front of my shirt and the tops of my shoes. I could feel the bread dough drying between my fingers, cracking like a second skin. I kept my hands behind my back so that I wouldn't have to shake their hands. The two men were young, nineteen I would guess, with short-cropped hair and acne. Their suits fit poorly, padded shoulders and pants unevenly hemmed. One wore black Reeboks on his feet while the other had a pair of scuffed wingtips. I saw no bikes, so I assumed they were walking their route that day, even though houses in the area were a good half mile apart. It must have taken a lot of energy to seek us out, the only non-Mormons for miles.

"This sure is a nice house," the Reebok-wearer said. He was apparently the one in the pair who had been in the field six months longer and was therefore senior. His twin looked around the yard, nodding his head. They each held the case carrying their leather-bound scriptures at their sides.

"Can we come in?" the senior missionary asked.

The fear I had nursed alongside my outsiderness had hardened into a shell of hatred by then, four years after our move to Zion. I had censored myself in the classroom, choosing books without profanity or sex; called the Preston library to complain that they were using taxpayers' money to buy books by Mormon writers when they didn't have a single book by Toni Morrison on their shelves; written a letter to the editor suggesting a staff writer had positioned women who had fallen victim to a rampant Peeping Tom as the ones at fault for not pulling their blinds. I was tired of waging what I saw as a battle, us against them. I was tired of the war.

"No," I said, "you can't." The porch boards creaked under the weight of the shifting missionaries, and the dough cracked on my skin. "And another thing," I continued, "I don't know why you think you have the right to come to my house, interrupt my day, my bread, whatever I am doing, and tell me what I should believe."

The senior companion began to object, held his hands up, took a step back.

"I don't come to your house! I don't travel halfway across the country to come to your house and tell you what I think you should believe. I don't say I think you treat your women unfairly. I don't try and persuade you to become a feminist or an environmentalist or a Democrat. I don't try and convince you to spend less time baptizing the dead and more time engaging with the world of ideas."

By now, the two missionaries, kids really, though at the time they felt like the machine itself, had backed away from the door. They didn't argue, didn't grow angry. They had been trained not to engage.

"How dare you come to my house!" I yelled, aware my voice was shaking. "How dare you knock on my door! Don't come back." My last words fell on their suited backs. Their rubber-soled shoes made hardly a sound on the sidewalks as they returned to the road. I watched them carefully latch the gate behind.

What causes two men to drive their pickup down the central street of a university campus yelling "Fag! Fag! Fag!" in the air? Who are they yelling at? Who do they hope will hear? I used to believe hatred caused such actions, pure, undiluted rage. But I have lived here long enough to understand the power of fear. Such behavior, I imagine, begins in the grocery store where bodies are concealed and sexuality is contained. It begins at the kitchen table where your father cracks gay jokes. It is furthered at school where the teachers allow kids to call each other "fag." It grows into a hot flame in the church pew on Sunday, where you are told that the door to eternity is narrow and policed, where the lines between lost and saved are engraved into your skin. All of that fear, anger, and repression must go somewhere. The energy cannot be contained. And so it erupts in ignorance and baseball bats, two men hurling hatred into the night sky.

I also understand the origins of hatred because of how bright my own anger glowed in the first few years I lived here. I understand how fear feeds on itself, becomes a dark and scary thing so that it suffocates any possibility of conversation, any possibility of change. Because the moment I slammed the door on the backs of the two missionaries, flour sifting to the floor and covering my shoes, I didn't feel vindicated. I felt empty. It would take several years for me to admit such sadness, an awareness of my complicity in perpetuating an us/them dichotomy. The acknowledgement of my own prejudice, of course, would begin with my students, individuals brave enough to share their stories.

Each semester several students in my creative nonfiction classes write about their mission experiences. Mission stories run the gamut, from the righteous to the rejected. The ones that break my heart are the ones by the students who have to return early from their two years of service and, therefore, return home without honor. Whether it is a sick family member, a psychological break, a health problem, or a crisis in sexuality that prompts their return, they arrive in my classes broken and ashamed. In their eyes, they have failed none other than God himself.

A few years ago, a student names Linda wrote about her bulimia, the way she struggled to hide her vomiting from her sister missionaries, a difficulty given that one rule of LDS mission work is that a missionary can never be alone. Linda was serving her two-year mission in Brazil, had learned a bit of Portuguese in the Missionary Training Center before being shipped thousands of miles from home to knock on doors and bear her testimony. She described the heat and the twisting vegetation around her. She described the days of rejection, doors slammed in her face, curses flung from windows like rocks. Amid the heat and loneliness, she took us into the bathroom with her where she purged every bite of apple, every piece of bread. With her, we ran circles on the tiny balcony above the jungle, laps to burn any calories that might remain. And when she was sent home a year early from her mission, we too could not meet the eyes of her family at the airport, shame soaring like a wind through our empty bellies.

An eating disorder is a slow suicide. The self-hatred necessary to stick your finger down your throat or starve yourself is a disgust I know well. In college I struggled with anorexia. I watched my body dissolve in my efforts to make it disappear altogether. I remember all too easily the shame of that disease.

So when I read Linda's story, I read it as one about the body rather than one about God. That Linda was a missionary mattered in terms of the limitations imposed on her, but those regulations seemed little different to me than the military culture in which I was raised. I had run my own laps. I had stood in front of the same mirror. In other words, I saw Linda as someone like me, rather than someone who scorned me. For once, it didn't matter what she or I did with our Sundays.

Such a realization didn't of course mean I then sanctioned the LDS church's enormous missionary undertaking or their stance on homosexuality. It didn't mean that suddenly I could read the local newspaper without anger. It didn't mean that my feelings about the church itself changed in any way. Rather it was just one of many moments over the years when I realized that the church and those who populate it aren't the same thing.

Brandon was in the same class as David last fall. Like David, he is gay. Unlike David, he has left the church. In his essay, he wrote about being noosed in high school and dragged around the auditorium stage by his neck because his peers suspected his sexuality. His journey out of the church began with his entry into the gay Mormon subculture, groups for LDS members who are gay and want to stay in the church. Brandon might tell you that these groups are the first step out, even though many are church-sanctioned. To gather that many gays and lesbians in one room creates too much possibility. Kissing becomes petting becomes oral sex and then, almost without realizing it, you are no longer in good standing with the church. In the celestial kingdom, your body will not be restored.

The essay Brandon workshopped last fall was about going on a mission and realizing he was gay. In the essay, he described in some detail a sexual encounter with another man. At the time, he was still trying to go to church every Sunday and much of the essay was about his inability to live a double life.

And there we sat, all of us, on a fall afternoon in a predominately Mormon state, twenty students: one an openly gay woman; one, David, a closeted gay Mormon; one, Brandon, a gay Mormon on his way out; and me, their teacher, who was learning that tolerance is a common act, meaning it arises from common, everyday interactions, around common and everyday things. And it begins with the individual.

Our classroom was physically small, the smallest in the building, so the semi-circle we formed with our desks was crowded and tight. At times, we touched our neighbor's elbows and ankles. When one shifted in his seat, we all shifted. In front of us, a common text, Brandon's essay. We each held a copy in our hands. The night before, we had all, in our separate houses, our separate rooms, read his lines together. The sex scene was explicit, pulsing with sweat and bodies and an underlying self-hatred. In his writing, Brandon did not flinch from the oral sex, even though, in class, I could feel his nervousness. Nothing I assigned in my classes ever approached the rawness with which he had written.

I began, "Okay, what do we think is working well here?"

Then silence, but not an unusual silence, just the silence of students thinking before they speak, the silence I equate with engagement.

"It's brave," one student volunteered, a woman, one who only days before, I imagine, had been sitting in church while church leaders warned against the evils of gay marriage.

"Brave, how?" I pushed.

"Well," she said, and looked up at her fellow peers. "What he writes about, his sexuality and his mission, most people wouldn't admit to it."

"So how does that help the writing?" I asked.

"We can't look away," she said. "It's like you always say about nonfiction. When you write about something true, something real, the reader can't look away."

Other students nodded their heads in agreement, several of them looking to Brandon.

He had given us something from his life, this small story, this gift, and having read it, none of us could ever be the same again. The following Sunday the LDS church might make another announcement about the immorality of homosexuality, but we would still carry Brandon's story with us. For a moment, the length of a breath, what was invisible had been seen for what it was. Nothing remained in the dark.

The other day missionaries came to our new home in Logan. When Aidan was three and Kellen a year old, we left our house near the cemetery and moved to town so that the boys would be in schools with more diversity and more options. This visit was the first time the church had officially called. We had chosen this neighborhood because it bordered the university. Most of those around us are still Mormon, but for the first time we actually know some of our neighbors. In fact the couple living next to us, Holly and Adam, are among the most open-minded and progressive people I have ever met. They attend church every Sunday. I imagine Adam will be a bishop someday. But I never think about their religion when we talk. Their beliefs do not shape our interactions any more than my vegetarianism does.

Snow fell the day the missionaries came. I watched them walk to our door, hoods held close to their faces. "The missionaries are coming," I said to Michael, who sat at the dining room table with the newspaper. "Will you get it?"

"No way," he said, and I too wondered if we should hide. But every light in the house was on, and I was standing at the kitchen window in full view of the street. Aidan and Kellen ran to the door when they heard the knock, jumping up and down at the possibility of guests on a cold winter's day. With their eyes on me, I opened the door.

"Hello," the pair said in unison, their shoulders fringed in white. Behind them, snow swirled in circles, revealing the invisible patterns of wind.

"That's a cool picture," one of them said, pointing behind me to the only slice of view I had given them into our house. "Where's it from?"

"The Spiral Jetty," I said, and then, in the same breath, "Look, guys, we have lived in this valley for ten years and aren't interested in being Mormon." I said it evenly, like I would tell a salesperson I wasn't interested in a vacuum cleaner or a new insurance policy. The statement was a fact, not an accusation.

I thought of Brandon on his mission, thought of David as well, thought of Linda running laps on her balcony and the path I wanted my sons to learn to walk as they grew up in this valley. Even though the two men stood before me in dark suits, white shirts, wore a name tag above their hearts that said they were from the LDS church, I didn't assume I knew them.

"Many of my students are missionaries," I continued. "And they write about the difficulty of knocking on doors all day long. They say how disheartening it can be, how lonely. I only want to be clear that we aren't interested in being Mormon." And then I paused, the cold air bright and clean against my face. "But I do wish you the best."

Kellen grabbed me from behind and pressed his body into my legs. Aidan danced in front of the plate-glass window.

"We just came by to borrow a cup of flour" one of the men quipped.

I laughed with them even as I shut the door; the furnace ignited in the basement. The pair walked down our sidewalk, dark coats pulled tight against snow that sifted from low skies. The flakes melted almost as quickly as they settled on the dark cloth.

Returned

Above you the sun strokes the late afternoon sky where gulls match shrieks with children, all punctuated by the surf. Even though it has been a year since you have seen it, you only glance at the sea, notice the pounding shore and the wetsuited surfers beyond. Michael walks beside you, Aidan and Kellen trailing like kite tails as you look for a spot on the crowded California coast, mid-March, a Wednesday, halfway through your vacation.

Turns out Disneyland is not the self-proclaimed "happiest place on earth," and the motel you booked online from Utah is not on the beach. The umbrella icon misled, for the beach sits several miles away by car. Not only must you drive but then you must pay to park. Nothing in California comes free, including the Pacific. Your ankles roll in the sand with every step, the cooler strap bruising your arm as it slides to your elbow. Each time the beach bag hits your hip, you curse Hotwire, Pixar, and the fact that you have to pee. The boys, three and five, carry shovels and buckets, asking to stop and dig every few seconds. "Here, Mommy?" they ask, pointing to a piece of sand claimed hours ago by a family of six. "Keep going," you yell, your voice lost in the crash of the waves. Why didn't you just eat lunch at the motel?

Kellen wears a bright blue suit and stumbles in the sand, his eyes on the sea rather than his feet, his hands clasping a bright green bucket to his belly.

An empty spot appears, and you drop the cooler, Michael landing next to you with a yellow bag of brand-new beach toys, a boogie board, and a sheaf of beach mats that remind you of your childhood in Hawaii. This isn't Hawaii. No one swims here except surfers in wet suits, too cold; the sand, coarse and gray. Still, it's the ocean, the Pacific, and the closest you're likely to get to Hawaii for some time. The salted air feels soft like you remember, and the moment before language leaves you, you feel the spray cup your cheeks like a hand. How is it again that you live in a state a thousand miles from here, landlocked and cold?

"Where's Kellen?" Aidan asks, pulling up to the chosen spot, shovel in one hand, bucket in the other.

For the first few seconds you are angry. Why doesn't he keep up? You have walked fifty yards from the parking lot, passed a hundred people, thin women in bikinis, blond surfers, mothers with children of their own, children who sit close to them building sand castles and eating salami sandwiches, children they can find. What you do not see among these bodies is your son, blue bathing suit, bucket with the tag still on.

Michael heads high, back in the direction you came, while you go low, to the sea, each of you obeying the demons inside without a word said to the other. You have lost him before, for twenty or thirty seconds, at the grocery store or the neighborhood park. He has always been returned to you, popped up from a tunnel or running down an aisle. Here, though, is the ocean. You have seen it fell tourists like trees. While you try to focus on the beach, thickets of people on towels and blankets, your eyes keep returning to the shore.

Waves crash again and again, white brew churning the sand, and you watch for bits of blue. You try to imagine what his body will look like when the sea has him, so you can know what to watch for. Will you see only a flash of suit, or will his whole body roll up the shore like the dead birds that often scatter the morning wrack line? The water will bite your skin when you go in, will burn, and the sea will try to take you deeper into its body. You can feel it pulling now. Fifteen compressions and two breaths, you think, quick for a child, your child, his lungs tiny, like a bird's, two puffs really, once you pull him from the sea.

But there is no blue, except for the blue of the sky, where the sun has burned the clouds away, leaving the sky like a bone picked clean. He is gone.

At first you try to keep your movements along the shore casual. You are not one of those parents. And you don't live here. Your winter-white skin, pale like the belly of a fish, pale like the tourists from Minnesota you mocked as a child, marks how long it's been since you stored beach mats in the trunk of your car. Every few seconds you look for Michael, expect to see his tall, thin body striding across the sand, holding Kellen easily in his arms, the green bucket banging against his shoulder. But Michael half-runs in and out of the beachgoers, his eyes panicked even from this far.

"Have you seen a little boy?" you ask a mother, who wears a brown bathing suit against even browner skin.

"What's he wearing?"

"Blue," you say (like the sky, like his eyes, like the ocean). "Blue."

Aidan searches halfway between you and Michael, tethered by both his parents, understanding, already, how attention can be lost. You do not need to worry about Aidan. He would never go near the shore. But Kellen?

And then you start yelling, because Kellen would, and the ocean is democratic in what it sweeps from the shore, a beach chair, a sea urchin, a three-year-old boy. To no one but everyone, you scream, "We just got here. He doesn't know. He doesn't know." Five minutes have passed.

You know what a small boy looks like when his lungs have filled with water. At eight, you saw Bryan, your brother, at the bottom of the pool in your backyard in Virginia. You had been left in charge, your mother in the house on the phone, the cord circling her body, leaving you under all those oaks.

You cannot say what happened. Perhaps he slipped with the acorns from the deck into the pool or maybe he tried to touch the reflection of the sky. While you jumped through inner tubes baked hot in the sun, he sank to the bottom where he lay on his back, diaper billowing. Under the water, bodies are magnified, their edges diffuse, and Bryan almost seemed to glow. If he had died that day, you would have thought he transformed into an angel right before your eyes.

But he didn't drown; instead your mother sucked the water from his lungs. So now what you remember is your mother's head thrown back to the sky, your brother limp in her arms, water rushing from their bodies to the ground, the deck spattered with red dirt.

You are running, sun pulsing above, ocean beating an angry rhythm at your feet. Running up and down the length of beach where you think a three-year-old's legs might carry him. Others look with you, or stand watching you run, their hands on their hips, eyes shaded. "Kellen! Kellen! Kellen!" you scream, your throat hoarse already. "Kellen! Kellen! Kellen!" So this is how your body will fail you, you think. It won't be your inability to drag him from the sea. You will simply run out of air. "Kellen! Kellen! Kellen!"

Ten minutes.

Michael will say later that he, a yogi, was praying the Hail Mary the entire time, over and over again as he searched near the parking lot, thinking Kellen must have been grabbed, remembering from some television show the first ten minutes are what matters in a child's abduction. Beneath the palms, behind the restrooms, in between rows of parked cars, he will recite the prayer of his Catholic childhood, the one offered up to a mother, a mother who lost her son.

You do not pray, but you beg the sky for his safe return. In those minutes, you want to believe that something larger than yourself is taking care of you. Because the ocean seems indifferent to your plight, hostile even, you have stopped looking for the fleck of blue at the foam near your feet. And the people on the shore only seem vaguely interested in helping. To them, you must appear like some kind of oddity, something the sea coughs up from its belly that you can't quite discern amid the driftwood and shell bits. A wild, crazy mother screaming to the sky. Your only hope lies in something greater than what you see before you.

Which is, right now, a group of college-aged kids playing football in the surf. They are drunk. Spring break. Plastic cups holding shots are lined up like a firing squad on a nearby picnic table. The waves crash into their bodies, sending white spray up their backs and into the sky. Madly, they fall on top of each other or the ball, hair soaking wet, thick strands matted to their faces.

They are saying something to you, something you can't understand. They are pointing and shouting, and then falling down into the surf. Their words mean nothing. "What? What?" you say, still running of course, dodging the water and their football, the cups wobbling on the table. But when they answer, it makes no sense. They yell again, but the sounds arrive garbled, unsorted.

You have entered another land, while they remain on the shore. And your language requires translation. You recognize the new place immediately, recognize it solely by the fact that you are the only inhabitant. The sky still serves as a canopy above you, but the waves have retreated, taking their ferocious noise with them. You have arrived in what poet Mark Doty calls "the land of limit and sorrow," and the emptiness prepares you to live without your son.

The spring-breakers continue to point down the beach, laughing, bodies bumped by each other and the waves. They drift away, merge into the froth, hair now strands of seaweed, skin salted and white, taking their youth and their Jägermeister with them. Aidan wanders on the shore still. You can see his red bathing suit, the sharks swimming above his shins, but he moves beyond reach as well. He is on his own. Michael will take care of him. You stop yelling. No one can understand you anyway.

Ahead of you, on the beach, a Jeep has stopped on the sand. The red flag waving from the back indicates a lifeguard, and you follow the tracks along the shore. The sand is cool within the path made by the tires. Grateful for the trail, you follow, no longer responsible for deciding whether to move high or low, to turn this way or that, knowing that with every turn, every decision about where to set your eyes, Kellen could be passing in the opposite, carried by the surf or by a stranger, just out of sight. A kind of frantic peace settles on you, the knowledge that the worst possible thing the world can offer has happened to you and that such pain begins in your belly, not far from where you carried your sons. There is only so much beach, only so much surf; eventually you will run out of places to look. Your throat has already demonstrated its limits. Language has left with your son. The trail continues down the beach, moving you closer to the Jeep. It is all you can do to follow its path.

When your mother pulled your brother Bryan from the pool, she held him to her body on the altar of bent thighs. At eight, you stood nearby, your hands empty. "Oh God! Oh God!" she screamed to the sky, and crows carried her cries on their wings as they rose in black congeries from the oaks. Head thrown back, your mother begged the sky and you followed her eyes, past the tops of the trees, to the blue expanse above and its dark clouds of bird. When your brother sputtered his first cry, your mother collapsed with his body to the ground.

You arrive at the Jeep, shiny and black, chrome bumpers gleaming in the sun. A red flag with a white cross at the center is painted on the side. The trail ends at the tires.

Your footsteps must have slowed because Aidan now trots beside you. This part of the beach sits deserted, far from any parking lot. At night the surf rakes don't comb the sand, so rocks and seaweed litter the shore. Even the surfers don't come down this far; only shorebirds ride the waves. Sandpipers and curlews run near your feet, their feathers iridescent in the sun. The Jeep throws a shadow, dark and cool amid all this brightness. You pass through it on your way to the front of the vehicle, and there you find your second son. He stands holding his green bucket, his eyes on the ground.

On your knees, on your knees, on your knees, you gather his small body to your own. This is what he smells like, you think, this is how his body feels. The lifeguard found him wandering the shoreline and radioed in the whereabouts of a blue-suited boy with curly brown hair. You didn't know this, but he had been found for some time. That's what the spring-breakers had been trying to say. That's why they were pointing. While you wandered in the land of limit and sorrow, Kellen was being watched over. When you raise your eyes to the lifeguard, you see only the blinding halo of the sun behind his head. "Thank you, thank you," you say to the lifeguard, the halo, to the sky beyond.

You say it again and again because there is nothing else to say. And then you rise with Kellen in your arms and carry him the entire length of the beach, thinking you will never put him down again, wishing him back into your body. Onlookers meet your eyes and smile. You had been screaming past them moments before, and now they seem genuinely happy that your arms are full. They hold, you think, their own children closer, walk down to the shore break hand in hand. Later you will learn the lifeguard's name is Bryan, like your brother. And while you will not know whether to place your faith in the universe, other people, or the natural instincts in a boy that have evolved to keep him away from dangerous surf, you will find comfort in the knowledge that even at the darkest hour, not everything may be lost. That night you will sleep with Kellen, keeping a hand on his body until the sun finds you both in the morning, returned to this world. "Kellen," you will call, softly now, "Bryan," you will say. And that will be a kind of prayer, and that will be enough.

The Little Bear

For Michael

We put in at a bend on the Little Bear River. While the boys chased a marmot back into its hole on the steep banks, Michael and I wrestled the canoe from the top of the van. Mid-April in northern Utah, the temperature dropped ten degrees each time the sun slipped behind a cloud. Daffodils and crocus dotted the sides of the busy road, bobbing in the breeze. When I looked toward the Wellsville Mountains, I could see a raft of cloud heading our way and wished I had packed our fleece jackets.

The green canoe was awkward and heavy, and I tried to balance it on my head as we moved away from the van.

"You got it?" Michael asked when the canoe wobbled like a drunk.

I didn't answer, just swung it from my head to the ground, one swift motion that took all my strength. Once it was down, we began to drag it to the river.

"Put your life jackets on," I called to the boys as I loaded the canoe with the cooler, blankets, and paddles. Aidan and Kellen ignored me, poked sticks into the marmot's hole instead. "Life jackets," I said again, a spring gust taking my words.

Michael and I slid the canoe down the steep bank, rocks and gravel rolling under our feet. We were putting in just south of the bridge where the road crossed the river, and I could see abandoned swallow's nests fastened to the concrete. The swallows had yet to return for the season, but the red-winged blackbirds called from the brush, high-pitched shrieks and trilling whistles, a welcome and familiar chatter, one of the first signs of spring.

"You know," I said to Michael, "you should wear the other life jacket, not me. If anything were to happen, you would need to help us."

Michael guided the canoe into the water like he might return a trout to the river, channeling the body through his long fingers, slowing the slide.

"You wear it," he said, as he steadied the canoe against the shore. Then he turned to call the boys. "Aidan and Kellen, hop in. It's time to go."

And because it was cold and the life jacket would be one more layer, and because the canoe was already pulling to be off, and because the boys needed help boarding the boat, and because I knew that we were only wearing the life jacket to set an example, I zipped it on, the vest a welcome embrace.

Once aboard, we floated quickly under the bridge, the river wide and muddy. On the shore, trees in early leaf stretched over the water, forming a tunnel through which we passed. I sat in front, a paddle resting at my feet, while the boys, seven and five, sat on the bottom of the boat. The two-person canoe meant they didn't have seats but rather camped on a wool blanket that must have felt both warm and scratchy against their bare legs. Michael paddled from his seat in the back, gentle J-strokes that kept us in the middle of the current. When I turned to look at him, he smiled, the easy smile he always has for the natural world, as if by leaving behind the van he had come home.

Fifteen years earlier, before we had boys, or a van, or any of those tethers that cause you to go to bed early so you can face carpools, sack lunches, and endless whining, Michael and I canoed our *Green Heron* down the gentle waters of the Huron River. We would put in at sunset, when the Michigan sun punctured thick stands of maple and picnicking families packed up to go home. A bottle of wine, sometimes two, a paper bag stuffed with bread and cheese from the local deli, and two wooden paddles were our only gear. Michael would recite poetry from memory, Pattiann Rogers or Mary Oliver, as he navigated the wide channel. His choices grew more boisterous as we drank, so that an hour and a half into the trip he would be flinging Pound's "Winter Is Icumen In" or Larkin's "This Be the Verse" toward the stars. I loved that he knew poems by heart, that he carried Blake and Shakespeare and Dickinson with him, fleets of words he set to sail on the river, our canoe buoyed by metaphor and image and voice. I, on the other hand, had memorized my day planner, could name the aisle in the local grocery where you would find Cheerios, knew to the penny the amount in my bank account, as well as the seven ingredients found in the Seafood Pita Pocket I sold as a teenager when I worked fast food. Because Michael brought art into the natural world, it meant every hike, every canoe trip, every backpack became laced with lines in pursuit of the transcendent. Our canoe, both boat and metaphor.

Usually at least once on our night floats down the Huron, often when the last shreds of light appeared like window panes between tree trunks, we would round a bend in the river and surprise a great blue heron. Prehistoric and heavyset, the giant bird would take off from its perch, tucking its claw-like feet against its body, and move slowly into the air, annoyance in every beat of its wings. Seemingly to make a point, it would often oar toward us, low over our heads, and then turn downstream to roost once more. A moment later, another bend, and the same heron would take flight again. We repeated the pattern several times, could anticipate the feathered whoosh of air above our heads, until, at last, the dinosaur of a bird flew upstream rather than down, leaving us in the Michigan night.

We would remain silent in the canoe for a long time; not even poetry could capture such encounters.

As we floated down the Little Bear, April sun lost behind clouds and the yellow-headed blackbirds sounding their alarm, I thought of those many canoe trips. How Michael courted me with poetry and rivers, so that his veined heart became the channel I followed, how we heaved the canoe and our drunken bodies up the shore and lay in the heron-plumbed blackness looking for the moon, how we never imagined we might, fifteen years later, paddle the same canoe down a western river with our boys (hearts now outside our bodies), sitting between us. In Michael's smile, his easy strokes, those rivers all ran together, so that this moment in the spring sunshine, quiet babble of boys, drill of bird, bob of tree branch, unfolded under the same "bones of the sky," "the meticulous layering" not of down but of memory, Rogers's redbird right there with us.

"Who's ready for lunch?" I called and reached for the cooler, unzipping the top.

"Me! Me!" Kellen shouted. He rose on his knees and the canoe wobbled, his forty pounds enough to shift the boat.

"Whoa," said Michael, "Careful." I watched him switch the paddle to the other side of the boat to stabilize the rock. "No sudden movements."

Aidan reached to pull Kellen back to the floor of the boat. "You're gonna tip us."

As usual, Kellen ignored his older brother and held out his hand for a slice of cheese, though I noticed he kept more still this time. I passed Aidan a wedge of cheddar as well as some crackers and a small bunch of purple grapes. "Share."

Michael and I only tipped our canoe once, during our trip to Algonquin Provincial Park in Canada. We had headed to the waters to celebrate the completion of Michael's PhD, the *Green Heron* strapped to the top of his Honda Accord, our clothes and food stuffed into rented dry bags.

The McKaskill Lake Ranger Cabin sits in a stand of red pine on a peninsula deep inside the park boundaries. To make our way there, we would have to put in at the Shall Lake Access Point and then paddle across several large bodies of water, as well as portage the canoe for miles between lakes. Because Michael had been busy defending his dissertation, we had not done the research necessary for such a long trip. Had we, we would have realized that such a journey calls for a light, Kevlar canoe, something one person could carry easily on his shoulders. We arrived at the park entrance at dusk, our heavy fiberglass canoe atop the car.

Because we had already driven two days, and because we had no money to rent a Kevlar canoe, we camped by the trailhead and set out early the next morning. At first, the two of us carried the canoe by the handles at either end, our dry bags the cargo. But my arms quickly grew tired and the progress was slow because we had to keep stopping in order for me to switch hands. As the sun vaulted the noon hour, we grew worried that we wouldn't make the cabin by nightfall. For the rest of the day, Michael carried the *Green Heron*, all seventeen feet of it, on his shoulders, plus a dry bag on his back. Mosquitoes swarmed his face and neck, their black bodies dark against his skin. He didn't have a hand to swat them away, so they feasted on his arms, his neck, the soft skin below his ears. Scrambling behind with the other dry bag, trying not to trip on root and rock, I could hear Michael pant from the exertion. He didn't talk, didn't make a sound. August heat pressed like wet washcloths to our faces. One foot in front of the other, five hundred yards, a mile, then canoe across open water, then shoulder the burden again.

I didn't think we would make it, couldn't see how Michael could keep going, but eventually we arrived at McKaskill Lake and canoed across the water to our cabin. I knew it was bad when Michael suggested feigning a broken leg so that a helicopter could take us back out.

Those days at the isolated cabin were amazing, though, a refuge amid miles of old-growth forest, trees that took root when Shakespeare was alive. Every night we fell asleep to the ghostly call of loons and listened to the moose forage outside our windows. During the day, we hiked or paddled around the remote lakes, drinking unfiltered water through cupped hands. The day before we left, we tipped the canoe, right at the shore when we were climbing out for a picnic lunch.

"We should never have tried to board when it was crosswise to the shore," Michael said, as we stood, completely shocked and soaked in knee-deep water. "That was dumb." But we laughed because it was only water and the cabin was close and soon we would be dry in front of the roaring fire.

I didn't think about Algonquin as we headed down the Little Bear, though we sat in the same canoe that Michael had carried. Instead, I studied the light, how, when the sun did appear, the water, the leaves, the birdwing seemed illumined from within. I didn't worry about tipping or trekking or becoming soaked. On the drive to the Little Bear from our house, earlier that morning, I had realized that such freedom from danger and worry was a gift Michael had given me for years. He mentioned, as we drove to the Little Bear, that he wanted to check the conditions at both the put-in and take-out sites. In my head, I thought about how much Michael worried, too much, and how everything was always just fine. A moment later, though, I realized that I didn't have to worry because he always did. My peace of mind was a privilege. That I could float down the Little Bear handing out a picnic was possible only because Michael took responsibility for everything else.

Up ahead, the river bent. From where I sat the river appeared to end altogether, the turn was so sharp. I knew at some point we would float under a great blue heron rookery, and I imagined for a moment seeing one of the giant birds rise from the shore as we made the turn. The bird would be larger than either Aidan or Kellen, with a wingspan as long as five feet. Perhaps it would be holding a fish in its beak, waiting to gulp the silvery body in one piece down its elegant S-shaped neck. It would sweep across our heads, belly just feet above us, bearing both its lunch and our past.

As we approached the bend, though, I forgot about herons. The river grew shallow on the inside of the turn. I could see the round rocks on the bottom, green and coppery in the sun.

"Michael," I called. "It's too shallow. We need to move to the right."

I didn't like shallow water. Just the week before we had run aground in the Cutler Marsh and had to extricate ourselves from the muddy bottom. I was worried we would ground ourselves here in six inches of water, jam the rocker into the sludgy bottom. But I hardly had time to articulate that thought to myself let alone name the fear aloud when the current picked up and we swung around the bend, the calm river replaced with white water.

It was as if there were two different rivers. The one before the turn and the one after. What had been wide, shallow, and slow moving funneled into a narrow chute. What had been straight and easily navigable became a lightning-shaped series of turns. To our right, at the first tight bend, a giant poplar had toppled into the water, its crown and trunk blocking the river. Branches and limbs reached across our path and formed a cage of roots. We were headed straight for it.

Michael didn't ask me to paddle. He was too busy thrusting his own paddle into the water. I threw down the knife and chunk of cheese, grabbed the paddle. Within two strokes, though, I knew we were going to crash.

The morning we left our cabin in Algonquin, I recalled the temperature of the water when we had fallen in. Shelter and a fire had been close by, so our shivering matched our laughing as we ran for warmth. A storm threatened our departure, and I could feel the chill in the air. We could see the dark clouds gathering to the north of us, throbbing masses of gray, but we set out anyway, knowing we had to be back in Ann Arbor the following day. It wasn't until the final crossing, the largest stretch of water, that the storm really hit. As we had navigated the trails, Michael once again bearing the canoe on his back, and then oared the crossings, the hemlock and yellow birch around us swayed in the gusts, some rain making it through the thick canopy to land on our heads and shoulders. Now, though, the trees blurred together in the wind, sugar maple becoming hemlock, the forest thrashing like a many-headed monster. Rain and wind swept against us, somehow rising from our feet, air and ground no longer meaningful, the world turned into storm. Even if the other shore had been close enough to see, we would have been unable to trace its outline through the mess. Waves crested on the lake, white caps crashing into one another, a turning brew of water that merged with the wind and rain. No one else was around, the middle of the day as dark as night, hardwood trees thin lines of black around us.

"We'll go at an angle," Michael said.

My teeth chattered even though it was August, my shirt and shorts soaked as thoroughly as they had been the morning before when we tipped.

"We can't go straight across," he continued. "The waves will tip us. So we'll have to cut through them at an angle. We'll head north of our landing place and then cut back south with the wind and waves behind us."

Michael stood, the canoe on the ground near his feet, and motioned our path with his hand. Our dry bags sat between the yokes where he had strapped them down with bungees. Water ran down his face, rain most likely but also sweat from having carried the canoe so far already that day. He didn't even try to wipe it away. Instead he gazed out at the lake, calculating, I knew, how to navigate.

"Once we commit," he said, "you need to keep your head down and paddle as hard as you can. Don't look up. Don't stop. Just paddle with everything you've got."

I didn't need to ask him about the dangers. I knew from his tone that they were many and varied and most of them ended up with us going into the lake with our gear.

Head down and paddle, I thought, as I helped Michael push the canoe into the raging water.

Every stroke resulted in little forward movement. The winds thrashed against us, our canoe a prop on the stage of storm. I couldn't see the shore, only saw dark water capped with frenzied white, but I trusted Michael to carry us there. I kept my head down and paddled, short hard strokes, quick and powerful. The canoe pitched and tossed, pulled or guided I couldn't tell, but I just counted my stokes. Ten on this side. Ten on the other. Again and again. Short, deep, fast.

"Hit the deck," I yelled, dropping the paddle, and I threw myself to the bottom of the boat, taking the boys to the floor with me.

The front of the canoe plunged into the cage of limbs, where we stuck.

"I'm scared. I'm scared," Aidan started crying. And then Kellen, "I want to go home."

Chaos in the *Green Heron* as I looked up to see that Michael was bracing his arms against the limbs to keep the rest of the boat from being pushed further into the tangle of the downed tree. Water rushed past us, almost brimming the gunwales: birdsong replaced by the thunder of spring runoff.

"Michael, pull us out of here. Pull us out of here," I yelled. From my position on the bottom of the boat, underneath the yoke so I could hold the boys, I could only see a roof of limbs above us. The water churned beneath the boat. I could feel the madness through the fiberglass hull. The river wanted the boat; all pressure bent in that direction, into the tree, into the river, down.

"Break some branches," Michael yelled above the fray. "Someone is going to be impaled."

I tried. I used my foot, my hands, all I had, but I couldn't break even the smallest of the limbs. It was a big tree; the river had already taken anything dainty or thin.

"Michael, get us out!" I cried.

He continued to brace his arms against the limbs, trying to back the canoe against the pull of water edging us forward, but we didn't move at all. There was no way back.

The boys were panicked now, crying and begging to leave the boat. I couldn't see their faces to reassure them, couldn't turn my body around.

"Michael, you have to stop and think. You have to be the one to free us." I could see his face, the strain of his arms against the thick branch. I looked at his eyes, which weren't panicked but purposeful.

"The only way out is through," he yelled. "We have to go through."

Which is what the river wanted, to carry everything with it on its journey north. I looked at the thicket before us and could not see a path.

Undaunted, Michael began to weave the canoe through the cage of bare limbs, using his arms to push against the tree limbs and moderate our exit. But nothing was gentle in the river, nothing slow, nothing quiet. We surged against the bulk of the tree, ducking branches and limbs, Michael guiding us as best he could from behind. Never once had he left his place on his seat. The three of us cowered at the bottom of the boat, but he stayed where he was, worked the limbs like a puzzle.

We popped free on the other side of the poplar, the canoe bursting into the rapids. I scrambled to my seat, grabbed the paddle once again. Our speed increased with our freedom. We didn't even cheer our escape. Now back on the main part of the river, still in the narrow, twisted chute, the current took us up again, a dropped stitch, a forgotten plaything, the third strand of a braid. Within seconds, the river swept the canoe into the second turn where the limbs of a bushy willow reached into the river.

"Short strokes," Michael yelled. "Short strokes."

It was the last thing I heard before the canoe tipped over.

The fall before we went to Algonquin, Michael and I took the *Green Heron* up north to the Au Sable Forest to canoe Rifle River, a sixty-mile stretch of water in northern Michigan that is popular for canoes because there are no dams or portages. We camped along the banks under an October sky compressed to the brilliance of a gemstone. Days before the trip, I had told Michael that I loved him for the first time. I could not help but read the carnival of color that surrounded us—maples in every shade of orange and red, birch like flames, honeyed cottonwoods, yellow ash, all backed by the cloudless blue sky—as a celebration of my happiness. On our third afternoon, we put in a few miles up from our tent site. Even though it was the second weekend in October, we wore short sleeves and hats. The sun warmed my skin. Michael sat in the back and paddled while we made our way down the lazy river. Curled leaves in yellows and red, tiny boats, floated alongside us, spinning in the current.

"Let's do that too," Michael said, when I pointed out the leaf armada.

I looked at him, confused.

But then he took his paddle and placed it on the bottom of the boat. Carefully he stood up and stepped over the yoke closest to him.

"Come on," he said.

Realizing what he meant, I waited for him to lay his long body on the bottom of the canoe. Even though the length from bow to stern was seventeen feet, the inside dimensions were much smaller, so Michael's body stretched almost from the back seat to the front. But the *Green Heron* was wide, a stable canoe meant for easy travel, and there was plenty of room beside him. I got up carefully and made my way to his side.

Then the two of us lay in the bottom of the *Green Heron*, blue sky above, the occasional burst of color as we passed maples and gums, curled fists of leaf falling through the sky, the canoe, bearing the two of us, bobbing down the river, bumping a bush, a limb, the shore, spinning in the water, just like the fleet of leaves surrounding us, the whole world adrift under an October sun.

When I came up, I saw Michael first. He held onto the overturned canoe with one hand and Kellen with the other. Aidan was closest to me, and I reached for him. We were soaked and already panting from fear. The shore rushed past us as we headed down the river, the four of us moving as one.

"You're okay. You're okay," Michael reassured. I didn't look at his eyes to know whether he thought this was true. Instead, I counted our four bodies again and watched the shore fly past.

"You're okay. You're okay," he repeated like a mantra.

Aidan and Kellen's eyes were wide with fear. They gulped both air and water but said nothing. Whereas before, in the cage of limbs, they had cried out in panic, now, faced not with the possibility of danger but danger itself, they conserved their strength and kept their heads above the water.

After a microsecond, I felt the cold pour into my body. The river stole into my jeans and long-sleeved shirt, soaked into my socks and shoes, weighted me down. It felt like the river was inside me, that my very center had gone watery and cold.

Our breaths came faster now. Short, gasping puffs. Our bodies swung around the bend, the shore maybe ten feet away.

"Swim to the shore," I yelled. And I tried to make my voice confident and strong as the rush of water pounded in our ears, blocking every sensation except for cold. I wanted Aidan and Kellen to think we knew what to do, wanted them to trust that we would fix this. But even as I yelled for them to swim, I saw the shore streaming past and wondered how we would make it.

I took Aidan and pushed him in front of me, knowing Michael would take Kellen. Together, we began swimming for land. The rocks and branches were going by so quickly, I worried we wouldn't be able to grab anything. Even if we made it to the shore, I thought the current would slam us against the rocks or that a branch might take out an eye.

We got closer, the force of the current lessening as we grew closer to land. I could taste the mossy water as it splashed my face and mouth, felt the freezing drops on my lips and cheeks.

"Grab on," I cried, hoping that Aidan wouldn't hit serrated metal or sharp rocks, but willing to take blood for land.

"Pull yourself up."

Aidan reached for a rock and then another. I saw him set his feet against the bank. With slow movements, he slowly climbed from the river, and I followed, struggling against the pull of the freezing water. Every time I tried to place my feet down, the current would steal my footing. The rocks on the shore, chunks of concrete really, were hard and jagged, but I welcomed the solidity. I crawled from the water and then looked back for Kellen. Michael was pushing him up the bank only feet from me. With each shove, Michael's head dipped down into the water. It was then that I remembered Michael didn't have a life jacket. While the rest of us bobbed on the river's surface, Michael had held onto the canoe for support. I watched as he struggled to boost Kellen up, the other hand still holding the *Green Heron*.

Michael looked up at me as Kellen made his way to my side. Holding the canoe, he was in the water, five feet below me, his face white with cold.

"Let the canoe go, Michael," I called.

Aidan and Kellen shivered at my sides, my clothes sucked into my body, the sky now full of cloud. Michael looked up at me.

Then again, louder, "You have to let it go."

I watched him hesitate, watched him look once more at the *Green Heron* overturned in the water, half sunk. Then he let it go. It hurried away, the cooler, his wallet, our water bottles, and our paddles chasing quickly behind.

Maybe the reason Michael recites poetry whenever we are in the natural world, rather than, say, when doing the dishes or taking out the trash, is to attempt to narrate, to hold within the bounds of language, a kind of beauty, joy, fear that we will never completely understand. Much like love itself. Lines of poetry, image and metaphor, frame the encounter, just for a moment, pin down what shifts and changes before our eyes. The mountains, the woods, the rivers, never fully known, yet familiar in the ways they call to us, are caught in image. Suppose your father was a redbird, Pattiann Rogers proposes. Suppose that before you knew how to speak you knew the "slow spread of his wing." "Then," the poet continues,

> you would be obligated to try to understand
> What it is you recognize in the sun
> As you study it again this evening
> Pulling itself and the sky in dark red
> Over the edge of the earth.

Language fails us in both love and beauty; yet it's all we have.

I don't think it is happenstance that Michael and I fell in love under the flap of a heron's wings. Every river runs with certainty toward an ocean that will always accept it, and a canoe follows every turn. All you need to know about life, the fierce ties that bind us as well as the branches that will take you down, can be found between those shores.

The four of us stood on the banks of the Little Bear under a sunless sky. Wind whipped against our wet bodies. Michael had lost his glasses and couldn't see. The canoe and everything with it was gone.

"It doesn't matter what we lost," Kellen said, the first words any of us spoke, uttered as he watched his favorite hat and green water bottle sail down the river. "The important thing is that we all survived."

And that was, of course, true. It's indeed what I felt standing on the bank, the four of us holding onto one another, the boys without shoes, Michael unable to see, water streaming from our clothes. We had made it.

Later I would realize we had only been on the water for fifteen minutes before the canoe turned over; it felt like I had been paddling much longer, that we had lived our lives within the hull of the *Green Heron*. Shock set in and I would only vaguely remember walking for thirty minutes through a cow pasture full of mud and manure, each of us with one boy in our arms, falling repeatedly into pools of filth. We eventually made it back to the van and then home for hot showers and food. The following day Michael would return to the Little Bear to look for the canoe. After two solid days of searching, through bracken and thicket, bruises and abrasions up and down his arms, he would find it, wedged underneath a willow, still upside down.

He would enter the freezing water once again, this time held fast by a rope, and with the help of two friends, pull the *Green*

Heron to shore. Aidan will stand on the banks and watch the resurrection because we will want him to know that what is lost can be found. Kellen, though, will refuse to go, will have nightmares every night for weeks, will whimper in his sleep. And that will seem about right to me as well. I too will relive the moment when the world became water and the river ran through me, will spin alternative endings with boys trapped by the yoke, separated from us, Michael unable to keep afloat in the brew. Through my sons, I will hold terror and joy in my hands, left and right, one and the other.

When Michael returns home with the *Green Heron* atop the car, spring rains coming down hard so that both he and Aidan are drenched to the skin, I will run from the house to meet him. His smile will say everything, joy pulsing with rain down his face. And I will hug him to me, feel the rain and the river soak into my sweatshirt as well as the deeper warmth and solidity.

THE SKY WITHIN

Bowl of Vastness

I lost God and my first husband on March 5, 1995. Together they walked down the jetway at Honolulu International Airport and boarded a plane bound for Wisconsin. My ex-husband wore a Packers sweatshirt and matching baseball hat. God was dressed in the same white robes he had been wearing fifteen years earlier when I took Jesus into my ten-year-old heart in the Quonset hut that served as Sunday School on Pearl Harbor. Over the next few months, I awaited calls from both God and my soon-to-be ex-husband, hoping they would return to me. Sometimes the phone rang. More often, I sat in silence. The last time I hung up, I was sitting on the tiled floor of the lobby in the Ilikai Hotel, the cord of the pay phone garroting my neck.

"I can't do this any longer," I said.

For the next decade I didn't hear from either of them.

That April, when I went to the registrar's office at the University of Hawaii to submit my name change form, the secretary congratulated me on my wedding. She would be the first in a long line of people I would need to correct.

When Kellen was born with immature lungs and had to spend his first nine days in the NICU, more tube and wire than baby, I prayed.

"Please let him be okay," I said, leaning against the incubator, three in the morning, bottle of breast milk still warm in my hands from pumping.

I did not call upon the white-robed figure of my childhood. He had spent far too long in the north woods fishing. I held no picture in my head as I begged the ceiling for a reprieve. The words dissolved like salt in the currents of the NICU, the lapping ventilator, the beeping oxygen monitor, the faucet turning on, then off.

Angels arrived in the form of nurses who did not wear white but rather colorful scrubs and Dansko clogs with socks in neon bright. They reassured me at every shift change that Kellen was going to be okay—not in words, though they offered me those—but more in their careful actions, the practiced grace with which they moved his arms, changed his diaper, carried him to the scale.

One morning I arrived to find a small black speaker in the incubator with Kellen, set near his head. A soft double whir pulsed from the box.

"What's that?" I asked David, our favorite nurse.

"Oh, I brought it for Kellen. It replicates the beating of the mother's heart. So he will feel safe."

I noticed then that Kellen had tilted his head just slightly toward that tiny mechanical heart, turned his bird-body toward the known. The whir coming from the speaker sounded exactly like the beat of his own heart when it first swam through the ultrasound at twenty-weeks gestation and confirmed his presence in a way no blurry image ever would. We took the ultrasound photos home and put them on the refrigerator. Within a few days, we could no longer remember which wisp of white was his arm and which his foot. The sound of his heartbeat, though, never left me.

That day, I stayed with Kellen, only able to soothe the parts his body not covered by tape or wire, and tried to recall the sound of my own mother's heart, a beat that I must surely know as well as my own.

We sat in a circle, five of us, black meditation cushions strewn about the room like fish left stranded on the shore. At the Cache County Jail, blue was the new black. Beneath their jumpers, the women wore T-shirts, orange Crocs on their feet.

"It's raining out today," I told them. Our time together had just begun. I had chanted a *shanti mantra*, seeking protection while we gathered, and the final *Om* still resonated in my chest.

"The clouds are gray and fill the sky. You can't even see the mountains." Each week my weather report arrived with my empty palms. The inmates had no windows, could not see sun or cloud. I was not allowed to bring anything into the jail except the news from the sky.

Brianna spoke: "Last night when I came back from dinner, all the women in my pod were sitting with their ears to the wall."

"What were they doing?" I asked.

"Listening to the rain against the building. You can hear it if you press your cheek to the concrete. We didn't know if it was rain or hail, but we sat there until it ended."

At that point, they had not been outside for five weeks.

"It was beautiful," she said.

"The rain?" I asked.

"No, all those women with ears pressed to the wall."

Right before God left for Wisconsin, I went to a reading at the Episcopal church in downtown Honolulu. Madeleine L'Engle spoke. I hadn't read any of her books, but I was keen to join St. Andrew's Cathedral, and they were sponsoring her visit. We gathered in a building adjacent to the cathedral itself, so I wasn't sitting in the room shaped like an inverted hull and built to the biblical dimensions of Noah's ark. Instead, I imagined such vaulted space.

At the end of the lecture, I asked her a question.

"Can I be a writer if I have never suffered?"

"Write," she said. "The suffering will come."

In 2014 I traveled to India for the first time with Michael and the two boys, who at the time were eight and ten. We lived for three months on the side of a mountain just beneath the peaks of the snowy Himalayas. Several days a week, I made the uphill trek to a cement studio where Vijay Amar taught yoga. At the beginning of class, we would sit in *sukhasana*, easy-cross-legged pose, with our hands to our hearts.

"Listen to the teachings," he said at the start of every class. "Be a better human being."

I never entered a church in graduate school. God had become another construct, another feeble attempt by human beings to make meaning out of chaos. He fell by the wayside along with Truth and Authenticity and anything that began with a capital letter. "Until death do you part," a speech act, I saw now, nothing more. My marriage vows along with Truth and Love kept company on the side of the road. I banked my heart like I would a fire every time I entered a classroom or opened a book. I learned to live in my head.

I began my PhD in 1995, months after I hung up the phone in the Ilikai Hotel. In my orientation, a senior doctoral student let us know that nothing existed outside of language. This included beauty and the divine. If it couldn't be articulated, it didn't exist. "Everything is a text," he said, quoting Derrida. He added, "It's all there to be read and decoded."

I wore a lot of black, drank coffee, and believed language made reality. Having abandoned the well-trod path that led to a min-

ivan and soccer games, I understood, in a way many of my peers
didn't, how words could shift and slip and move beneath you.
One day your husband simply says he no longer loves you. Not
unlike marriage itself, reality was partial, halting, and temporary
at best. Nothing was eternal.

Moving to Zion after graduate school should only have served
to confirm my atheism. Living in a theocracy, having your home
address determined by your exact distance from the Mormon
Tabernacle, impels you to mark yourself as other: tattoo your
knuckles, bare your shoulders, visit the state liquor store fre-
quently, bring your coffee with you to teach. When the majority
around you belong on the inside, you begin to take pride in your
outsider status. You don't want anyone to mistake you for anything other than Other. You do not go to church, any church.
When your son is a year old, you have a woman in Spain pierce
a helix along the edge of your right ear, in a place where the
cartilage receives little blood, and the hole never entirely heals.
When you turn the silver ring, you relish the pulse of pain.

But then.

You walk outside your door every morning. And the mountains lift their shoulders toward the sky. The sun rises from behind
the peaks and throws limbs of light to the ground that seem solid
enough to scale. The air smells of pine, and the flowers that arrive
in the spring are so hard-earned you crumple at the sight of their
fragile heads. The poet asks: why this and not something else?
You find it hard to cling to the sterile shore of atheism when
nurses lay your heart next to your newborn's head, and the world
arrives not as a void or darkness or rubble but as a mountain ash
with limbs that fountain fifty feet above your head and leave you
in its shade.

"Clouds alone," Michael once told me, "are proof enough for
me of the Divine."

One Monday before the winter solstice, I led the women at the jail in a guided meditation. We began by imagining a ball of light in our bellies, in our wombs. A seed of light, I told them, but one connected to us, umbilicaled and held. They were, I said, in the midst of a double winter, but the promise of renewal was not far away. Days would be growing longer now, the darkness, lessening.

Over the course of ten minutes, we enlarged the reach of that light. First it filled our bellies, then our bodies, then the room.

"Feel the light move under the door," I suggested. "All the light now pushing beneath the sill."

With our eyes closed, we envisioned the light moving down the metal stairs to the floor below us, then out the door, not needing a buzzer, permission, or accompaniment. I asked them to think of this light merging with the sky, becoming one with everything and connecting us all. In that windowless room on a day with more dark than light, we awaited the spring.

At the end of the meditation, I wanted to give them all a hug. In a few days it would be Christmas, and they would be spending it in jail. I knew they had made cards for one another, gifts hidden from the guards. Brianna had spent the little money she had buying each woman in her pod one piece of candy from the canteen. "For their pillows in the morning," she had said.

Moving toward the door with its buzzer that would release me into the wintry afternoon, I didn't hug them. Last year, one of the volunteers had embraced a prisoner he hadn't seen in months. No rules forbid such contact, but the guard didn't like it. The volunteer was not chastised, but the inmate was thrown in the Hole.

"I miss the sun," Brianna said, "and a brush. We're only allowed a comb."

We like to think our lives unfold along a line that can be traced, a narrative that makes sense, with a beginning, a middle, and an end:

Once I believed in God. I prayed to him. I was a good girl who didn't drink or swear. As a child, I served as an acolyte who lit the altar candles with the solemnity of a portrait. I remained on the kneelers until I confessed every sin I could imagine and then confessed the ones that came to me as I imagined sin. But the story fell apart and God didn't survive the retelling. First because he packed his bags, and then because there was no rational way to explain his existence. If reality narrows to what we can name and know for certain, then the idea of God very quickly becomes the stuff of fairy tale. The end.

But not even our days travel such paths, let alone a lifetime. I am old enough now that I can see the arcs my life has taken, install climaxes, find the metaphors. Viewed from certain angles, the story satisfies like a well-made dress. And yet, I cannot fully explain to anyone how I have come to believe in the existence of a force beyond what I can name. The narrative thread unravels in the telling. Effect can no longer be anchored to cause. And this uncertainty feels far more fitting than the well-made dress.

Toward the end of graduate school I met Michael. An outlier in a black-clad throng, he was wearing a pink button-down when I first saw him at the copier. He offered to interrupt his print job for me.

A poet himself, he was writing on Whitman and conversion. His dissertation consisted of thousands of words trying to describe the indescribable moment when one touches the face of God. Conversion, a turning, away from and toward, always happened in an ecstatic moment. He studied the nineteenth-century culture of conversion but really what he studied were those men and women from the past who stepped forward with their heart in their hands and tried to explain what they had seen.

"Everything that really matters, love, loss, bliss," Michael said, "happens outside of language."

His dissertation had pages and pages of footnotes. Their sheer volume was evidence of something.

The first time we traveled as a family to India, we arrived in Mumbai in the middle of the night, though you wouldn't have known it from all the activity. People thronged the streets, gathering in the yellow glow of lighted tea stalls, drinking chai and scooping food with their fingers from paper bowls. Bollywood music flared from passing motorbikes. The absence of stars, eclipsed by the streetlights, left the sky flat and dull. Riding in the taxi with Michael and the boys, I felt like I hadn't seen the sun for days. As soon as we arrived in our hotel room, we collapsed on our beds, not even brushing our teeth.

Three hours later, though, I woke. After all, it was the middle of the day back home. I tossed and turned for half an hour before wandering onto the skinny balcony to absorb the unfamiliar sounds of this country—birds that cried out like humans, crickets and tree frogs, the constant scattershot of horns.

I wanted nothing more than to run. Having traveled for thirty-eight hours, my back and legs ached with inactivity. More pressingly, though, I was worried that India would become the first place I had traveled where I couldn't run. Every website we read, every book we borrowed, every native we asked had told us before we left that no one ran in India, especially Western women. It wasn't safe, or it wasn't appropriate, or it simply wasn't done.

Even though I had no idea what part of the city we were in and wasn't even sure I could make it from our room to the hotel lobby, I laced my shoes and headed out the door without a key.

No lights illuminated the hallways of the Mumbai hotel, so I kept a hand on the walls and walked carefully in the dark. Around a corner, I found stairs, which I followed to the lobby. Even though it was early, a man stood at the front desk, fully dressed in a suit and tie. He greeted me with a smile.

"Is there a place I can run?" I asked. I had been thinking I would say "walk" when I approached him, so that I didn't arouse any alarms. Given his formal dress, I felt out of place in my running tights and T-shirt. I waited for him to ask me to repeat my question or to send me back to my room.

The manager, though, didn't bat an eye, didn't even pause. I couldn't fully understand what he said, but it wasn't "You can't run here!" He had given me directions, and I clearly heard the word "beach." I stepped outside and turned left.

The sky had started to lighten from black to gray, though I couldn't see much past the canopy of trees. All along the sidewalks and into the streets, whole families slept on thin blankets. Most of them were still asleep, many on their backs, their hands folded across their stomachs. Children drew close to their parents, most without shoes or clothes. One couple held hands. I ran down the middle of street to avoid the sleeping bodies, listening for horns. When I came to the first intersection, I discovered a bridge over a set of train tracks. I remembered the manager of the hotel motioning up with his hands, so I headed for the stairs. An old man, bent and withered, slept at the landing. A tea stall with a red metal roof stood nearby, the owner just beginning to heat his chai. Although I could not read the Hindi on his sign, I thought I could find my way back to the rise of steam and smell of cardamom.

Across the train tracks and down the stairs, I passed another sleeping body. The road continued, so I ran down it. A cow was tied to a stake on one side of the road. On the other, someone had hammered a soap dish into the trunk of a tree. Crows hopped on the patches of dirt around me. Thin men holding buckets and tattered rags washed their cars. Each stride took me further from the known, and yet I continued down the shaded road.

Hanuman is the monkey god, the god of compassion. As a young monkey, he saw the sun and thought it a mango. He leapt for the yellow light, but Indra, worried he might take down the sun, threw one of his lightning bolts at the monkey boy. Hanuman fell to the ground and cracked his skull.

"The god of compassion comes to us broken," Hope concluded. "Something for us to think about as we practice."

My mother and I had joined Hope and ten other people on a retreat in Mexico a year or so after I first went to India. The morning she told us the story of Hanuman, we were gathered in a yoga shala set above the ocean, waves crashing a hundred feet below. "But that isn't the most important Hanuman story," Hope continued. "It only sets the stage." We moved into pigeon pose, and she continued.

Ram and Sita were lovers, but Sita was stolen and taken to the island of Sri Lanka. Ram sought the help of Hanuman in securing her return. Because Hanuman loved Ram dearly, Hanuman used his long monkey legs to leap the ocean and bring Sita home. In gratitude, Ram gave Hanuman a beautiful jeweled bracelet, but the silly monkey ate the gems.

"Have you no respect?" Ram asked him. "Have you no love?"

Hanuman looked up at Ram, broken jewels at his feet, and cut open his chest. On every vein of his heart was inscribed "Sita Ram."

"We are," Hope concluded, "every figure in Hindu mythology. We are the one who can leap and the one who throws lightning. We are the one who inscribes our love upon our flesh and the one who questions its limits. We are the remover of obstacles and the obstacles themselves."

She didn't need to add that we are also both monkey and the Divine.

When Kellen was a baby, he would awake with night terrors. We would hear him screaming in his sleep and run to his crib where he would be standing, holding the wooden bars in his hands, eyes wide open in alarm. But he wouldn't be awake.

"Kellen, you're okay," we would say, pleading in our voices. "Kellen, wake up."

We would pick him up, rub his back, bounce him gently in our arms. Sometimes we would shake him, try to rattle him into this world. But he would not awaken, even though his eyes were lit with terror. He would just scream, his body board straight, everything in his posture pushing us away.

The first few times it happened, Michael and I thought he was having a seizure. Kellen seemed almost catatonic, unreachable, the gaze of his eyes beholden to an inner terror that we could not witness with him. And he was inconsolable. In my arms, though not in my arms, he gave us no direction to even head. We could only wait it out, and the nightmare would last for minutes that felt like lifetimes.

I had no doubt that in these terrors he was reliving the first nine days of his life, needles in his scalp, ventilator down his throat, the womb not replaced by blankets and touch but hijacked entirely for an incubator made of glass and metal. And I blamed myself for putting him there in the first place, for my inability to keep him in my body longer, for failing to protect. Every time he woke screaming, I let his cries slice me, let his suffering wound.

Then one night when he was beyond my reach, wandering a landscape that he will never be able to describe, I took him outside, under the stars, in the kind of dark only possible when you leave the built environment of the city and live in the country. As soon as we stepped beneath the sky, he quieted. His body relaxed against mine, his crying ceased, and he returned to this world. Perhaps it was simply the change in temperature or the quality of the air that brought him back to us each time. Perhaps he would have returned that very moment even if we had been standing in the hallway. But it happened too many times for it to be so easily explained. In those moments wracked with terror, what was inside of him, I think, was absorbed by the vastness of the outside, the stunning fact of galaxy and a path of stars as thick as cream. When we moved outside, we actually moved toward something deeper and more fundamental. There is an ancient yoga text that encourages us to "enter the bowl of vastness that is the heart." Such a space, it suggests, has "no beginning and no end. Embrace this infinity without reservation. You are its vessel."

At the age of seven, I fell off the back of the couch in the basement and hit the cement floor. The fall knocked me unconscious, for how long will never be known because my parents were gone for the evening and the babysitter knew enough to lie. For several weeks, I suffered from double vision, seeing two of everything. But I didn't tell my parents. I should not have been standing on the back of the couch; a doubled world seemed just punishment.

Though my skull was not technically cracked, I certainly felt divided. Even the simplest of actions, putting a glass on the table, becomes impossible when you are unsure which image of the table is real. I walked sideways, couldn't go up and down stairs. Finally, my parents took me to the hospital where I was admitted within an hour.

At the time, Bethesda Naval Hospital had a floor for children who were broken, ill, and dying. I joined the ward that afternoon, my bed next to a girl in a full body cast. Some of the kids had shaved heads. One could no longer see. Once a week we gathered in the art room and worked with clay and paint. Surgery loomed in my future. The doctors could not keep my brain from swelling. I went to bed scared at night, worried I would not wake up, worried I would die.

Those long days in the hospital are held in memory like a leaf in a lake of ice—not so much preserved but isolated, set apart. Until then, I did not know how easily bodies could fail, how easily we break. The girl with the crossed eyes remains with me, continues to gaze out. She doesn't see double any longer, but she does feel cracked. While medically, the blood pushing on my optic nerve receded and my vision was returned, in my felt body I have never left behind the knowledge that while I am walking along the bread aisle in the grocery story another remains immobilized in plaster. Kellen will never entirely leave the incubator. I am held by something I cannot see or name. These realities are not so much parallel as layered, one on top of the other, not unlike the twin thumps of the heart.

Maybe if I had to name a moment, locate a place in my life where I realized how the heart sees by its own light, to quote another yoga sutra, I would return to an Easter morning in Santa Fe, when I entered an actual church for the first time since God's plane took off on the reef runway. I am not sure what compelled me to go to the St. Francis Cathedral that morning. Michael and the boys remained in Utah, so I was alone. Maybe I just had the time. Or maybe learning that it was the oldest Catholic parish in the nation made me want to go. Or maybe I wanted to see the stained-glass windows that had been carried by covered wagon. For whatever reason, I sat that Easter morning with hundreds of others to listen to the music and the prayers.

I arrived early, but the pews were already filling. Music played from an unseen organ, and candles lit the church. Light poured in through stained-glass windows, while ushers encouraged people to move toward the center. The ceiling rose above me, painted in white and gold, and statues watched over the alcoves along the sides. I took a seat on a tiny pew without a kneeler, the last open space that still afforded a straight line of sight to the altar. I placed my purse beside me and watched others arrive in their Easter outfits. Hats and gloves mixed with blue jeans. Children carried chocolate bunnies and jelly beans in their hands.

"Can I sit with you?"

I looked up to see a woman, older than me, pointing at the lack of space beside me. The pew, just a tiny bit of a bench near a column, could maybe hold two people if they snuggled, but two strangers seemed doubtful.

"You have such a good view," she said.

I put my purse under the bench and tried to make myself small. She slid in beside me, our thighs touching. I was annoyed. I had chosen this spot for the same reasons she had, its centrality, but in my head I judged her. Who comes to church, I thought, for the view?

The service began, and I followed along in my bulletin. The words of my childhood returned to me. The Creed and the Lord's Prayer rising up from some deeply engrained part of my past. Light shone from every surface and incense curled from swinging brass censers. When it came time to sing, the music eddied in the shadowed corners of the building, seemed to vibrate off the walls where Jesus wore his crown of thorns and offered his bleeding heart.

Beside me the woman sang. I could feel her voice more than hear it. Her arm pressed into mine, each exhalation a movement of her rib against my own. I glanced at her through the sides of my eyes, at the one pressing up against my body, taking my space. In India I would not have thought twice about such proximity, but in the U.S. I was annoyed she had come so close. I felt the fact of her, noticed her tennis shoes and dyed hair, her dress and the glasses she kept dropping on the ground. We are more alike than different I thought. True, I had hidden my comfortable walking shoes in my purse before entering the church, and I only needed reading glasses for medicine bottles and recipes on the backs of packages, but there was such little distance between us. We both wanted the view, the contact, the music, the light. And all of that did not so much exist around us as within us. The Divine was sitting next to me in sneakers. I just had to make room for her.

Mumbai is a city of seventeen million people, and on my first morning in India I was running somewhere in the middle of it. My route had not been straight, or signed, or known. I kept trying to focus on landmarks that would lead me back to the hotel—there a purple shrine, there a bus stop with a serpentine roof. Rain trees arched over my head. Morning light shone behind the leaves and limbs, embroidering the sky. The trees reminded me of Hawaii, my childhood home. For entire afternoons, I had played in their shade, climbed their branches, swung from their limbs. When I breathed in their smell, for a moment, India felt familiar, known.

Three blocks later, the street opened into white sky. As I ran closer, the air grew denser, and the soundscape deepened. At the end of the tunnel of trees, I emerged on the Arabian Sea, a sweeping expanse of ocean reaching in all directions. Narrow streets and unknown turns ended in an explosion of ocean and light. The sun, now up, threw beams of orange and yellow across the waves. Birds landed on the stone wall and then lifted just as quickly. The sky matched the sea in hue.

Scores of Indians were out exercising on the broad promenade. True, most of them were walking, most wore saris or long pants, and no one was dressed like I was, but they were all out there, swinging their arms, listening to music, sweating in the ninety-degree heat. I crossed the street and merged into the throng of bodies. The sea rose and fell at my feet like a chant, the rising sun glinted orange on the skyscrapers, and my legs savored every stride. Joy came in the familiar fall of my feet on the ground and the knowledge that, while I stuck out in my white skin, gray Nikes, and red T-shirt, no one even questioned what I was doing. I was making my heart known in my body, the double thump in my chest, the echo of Kellen's heart as well as my mother's, the beat I had never lived without. We all were.

Taxi Sutra

The Reality is one and the same: the
difference is in name and form.

—Sri Ramakrishna

Six weeks into our three-month stay in India, a taxi ran over Kellen's foot. I will never forget the sight of his shoe pinned beneath the tire. The day had started quietly. By that June morning, we had lived a month and a half in the tiny town of McLeod-Ganj, high up in the Himalayas, where ten-thousand-foot peaks stood garbed in snow even in mid-summer and the walk to town for groceries required a perilously steep ascent.

We left the cottage around nine that day, hoping to beat the sun. For the first time in our stay, we turned to go downhill toward Dharamsala rather than up to McLeod Ganj. Recently, we had learned about a Domino's Pizza at the top of the town and told the boys it would be a Friday treat. The boys ran ahead, their legs, for once, in tune with the pull of gravity.

The road to Dharamsala was paved, though broken, uneven, and narrow. When the small cars, auto rickshaws, or motorcycles would scream through, we made sure to step to the side. Above, the cloudless sky stretched over our heads and threaded the nearby jagged peaks. On days like this it seemed like we lived inside a castle, with a mountain turned turret and jewels for a ceiling. For moments I could forget the poverty that pulled at our hearts every day, the path to town lined by those asking us for money, those missing limbs, missing parents, missing sight. Walking downhill that morning, sky and mountain all around, I focused on Aidan and Kellen skipping down the slope and the bulbuls and macaques calling from the trees, inviting us to join their raucous celebration in the limbs of the cedars.

The *Yoga Sutras* were gathered by Patanjali some two thousand years ago and bound into a text that feels less like a map for the practice of yoga and more like a series of unsolvable riddles. The Sanskrit word *sutra* is cognate with "suture" and translates into thread. Containing 196 aphoristic phrases that range from the practical—how to sit while in meditation—to the sublime—the esoteric distinctions between two stages of enlightenment—the sutras attempt to thread together or bind yoga, one of the six schools of classical Indian philosophy. Most yoga practitioners in the West have never heard of Patanjali's sutras. Of the sutras themselves, less than one percent are dedicated to the practice of asana, the poses that make up the center of what westerners call yoga. Patanjali himself, and yoga more broadly, was barely concerned with the position you took when you practiced (the word *asana*, which most think of as a pose in yoga, really means seat). Instead, his focus and the focus of the sutras is *moksha*, liberation—freeing the soul.

I have long appreciated where Patanjali begins the sutras—with *atha*, the Sanskrit word for "now." And beginnings are important in such works, for in most classical Indian philosophy that which comes first, say in a list, is considered most important. For example, when Patanjali turns his attention to the *yamas*, the ethical practices a yogi should follow, he lists *ahimsa*, nonviolence, as the first of five. The commentators over the centuries have stressed the centrality of nonviolence to yoga practice—from that, they suggest, stems the rest. It seems, therefore, keenly important to consider the first word in the entire work he has undertaken: now. Now, he tells us, is the time for yoga.

In a single day last week, five students cried in my office. I teach memoir writing to graduate and undergraduate students—classes where I ask them to push hard and explore difficult questions—so it is not unusual for students to reach for the Kleenex during office hours. They are writing about complex and often painful subjects. Most balance work and families as well as school. They are in debt, unsure about the future.

Still, five in one day is a lot: a woman who had been raped by a family friend at the age of nine and now battled bulimia as she tried to rid her body, ten years later, of the pain; a gay man who had to leave the Mormon church in order to live with the man he loved and now asked how God could have abandoned him; a woman who served in the Army Reserve and felt guilty that she hadn't put boots to the ground while her best friend had been killed guarding a dinner party in Iraq; another young woman who could not lift her hoodie to show me her eyes but instead gnawed on her fingers, nail beds raw and bleeding; last, a woman trying to come to peace with both her abortion and her rape.

I have been teaching college students for fifteen years. The trauma, anxiety, and depression that mark their lives seem to have increased in the past decade. Students on medication, treatment plans, shattering in front of me as they describe what they want to reveal in their art. I carry their stories home with me every day; I read them over the weekend; I send them love in the predawn hours when I take a seat on my meditation cushion and try to quiet my mind.

But lately I have trouble maintaining my center. The heft of their stories keeps me awake at night, presses on my chest, cannot be quieted by breath.

India was never quiet. It challenged all of us every single day. Part of the bribe to encourage Kellen to walk to Domino's was a taxi ride home. When we had first arrived in India, we warned the boys that leaving the comforts of the United States would be difficult. Actually, Michael warned them. He had already been to India three times and knew what to expect. "Heat," he said. "Noise," he said. But you really have no idea.

After our first excursion to see the Gateway of India in Mumbai, Aidan, who was ten, returned to our air-conditioned hotel room and fleet of bottled water to collapse on the bed. He declared: "I am never going out there again."

But six weeks into our time in India, the boys had acclimated to the smells, the animals, the colors, the noise. Kellen hardly flinched when elderly women would come up to him and want to pinch his pale cheeks. Aidan grabbed a "monkey stick" as soon as we would enter the canopy of cedars to fend off the macaques, just like the locals. What they couldn't bear, the reason Kellen would beg us to stay home in the cottage all day and play games rather than face the walk to town for groceries, was the poverty. Really, none of us could bear it. Even now, two years later, I can close my eyes and see the man with no eyes calling "Namaste" at the sound of approaching footsteps, the woman bearing her baby and gesturing fingers to lips, the two toddlers in a cardboard box on the side of a road, the man whose scarred body had once, it seemed, been aflame. Every day our vast privilege was made painfully evident, and we found few ways to carry either our fortune or the poverty that surrounded us.

A taxi was a luxury, as was the promise of Domino's pizza. At this point into our stay, the boys recognized such things as gifts that many others did not have. Because we insisted that the boys walk everywhere—that is what we do in India, we said, we walk—Kellen gladly accepted the offer, and that meant we were out in the sun headed to Dharamsala. Given the heat, I think we were all thankful not to have to haul ourselves back up the hill.

We reached the town around eleven and stopped at a place for coffee and treats. While we waited for our food, we played Pictionary on sheets of paper I found in my bag. When the boys grew bored of that game, we scrambled words for each other to guess. Kellen stumped us all with "chalkboard," jumping up and down at his win.

Even though we arrived at Domino's well before lunch, the familiar smells of already baking pizza greeted us at the door. We put in our order and waited, talking about how good the pizza would taste.

Fifteen minutes later, we had a box with a large cheese pizza, which Michael held in front of him like a platter. We opened the door to the cry of horns, the crush of bodies, and the heat, leaving the word "chalkboard," the air conditioning, and the familiar blue-and-red logo behind.

Contrast binds yoga together—whether the literal tension found between crown of head and sitz bones in a seated pose or the pause between inhalation and exhalation. Patanjali's yoga, as a philosophy, presents a dualistic system, one that divides the world into the unmanifest and the manifest. Patanjali uses the term *purusa* for the never-changing, eternal unmanifest, that is, the Divine, and *prakrti* for everything else: the things of this world, our bodies, and, in contrast to the Western mind/body split, the mind as well. Often yoga teachers will translate yoga into union—or a yoking. The root, *yuj*, does mean to yoke, so the translation makes sense. When instructors define yoga this way, they usually give the yoking of the mind and body as the example, or the body and the breath, or maybe the body and the spirit. Through awareness of the breath and movement in the posture, one can, they suggest, unite the body and mind.

But the commentators of Patanjali's sutras, Edwin Bryant most recently, point out that yoga requires a *disjoining* of two things: by stilling the mind, one realizes that the body and the mind and the things of this world, the prakrti, are limited and changing and ultimately transitory. Rather than leading you to the Divine, they tend to imprison you—make you desire, want, and crave. Only by realizing the changeless purusa inside your self—the higher Self or even the soul—can a person escape the bonds of suffering (the endless desire for something other than what we have) and realize his or her divinity, which is, yoga tells us, our birthright. For Patanjali, the study and practice of yoga allows one to extricate the purusa, the soul, from the confines of prakrti. It liberates the Divine inside of each person.

Importantly, this realization does not arise from headstand or downward dog or warrior one, two, or three. *Viveka*, discrimination, comes from meditation: stilling your mind and taking your awareness into the present moment. It comes from settling into the now.

To the five students crying in my office last week, I want to add the friend of Jen's, a man not yet forty-five, who has two children and has just been diagnosed with stage-three cancer. I want to add my mother-in-law, who suffered a tiny stroke—when? while she was watering her bonsai? walking her dog? reading *The Poisonwood Bible*?—and now writes to me in cursive I can no longer read. I want to add Kellen as well, who hides in his closet and cries, telling me to go away. And then the women in the jail where I teach meditation, no older than my students, specifically the one who started crying when I suggested that she could be a teacher to herself, or maybe the one who broke down when she revealed that the prosecutors were recommending prison, as the fluorescent lights hummed above us, lights that blink and buzz and never dim, sunlight impossible, forgotten, withheld. I pile all these stories at the foot of Friday. I push them under my bed. I send them through the washing machine with the jeans and T-shirts. I sit with them in the car as I drive to the grocery store, where I will fail to remember my great good fortune as I walk down the brightly lit aisles full of food.

Maybe that is why Shiva, the god of destruction, has so many hands. Maybe that is why all the deities in the Indian pantheon sprout arms like branches, reaching to the sky. There is simply too much to hold.

I remember a story about demons overrunning the land. And how the villagers prayed to Shiva to save them from blackness and despair. He came down from the sky and took the demons into his body, but he didn't swallow them or spit them out or even end their lives. He just held them. With his many hands.

I like to think he is still holding them now.

Pizza in hand, we left Domino's. Outside, the temperature had cooled. Clouds gathered above us, and it looked like rain.

"It's not too hot," I said to the boys. "Let's just walk home." The exercise would be good for us all, I reasoned, allow us to "earn" the pizza we would eat in our cottage.

The protests were immediate. "You promised!"

Cars and cows and people swirled around us on the street. The clouds gave everyone the chance to slip from house or work to buy some groceries or chapatti or bunches of greens carried to town on backs from nearby fields. We walked amid the chaos, holding hands and listening for especially insistent horns. No matter the crowd, we always stood out as foreigners. Our dress, our skin, the way we flinched when a moped came too close. Which meant that if we even looked like we *might* need a taxi, several would veer in our direction. Most often, we shook our heads. "We can walk!" Today we actually needed one and none could be found.

Near an intersection, a man on foot approached us.

"Taxi?" he asked.

"Yes."

He gestured for us to follow him, and I thought he was taking us to his taxi, but instead he led us across the street, where he stopped on the side of the road and waved his hand.

A small white car appeared, and the driver inside smiled at us. The car was headed down the hill, and we needed to go up, but it was apparent by his emphatic gesturing that we should climb in and he would then turn around. Nearby, cars streamed past, maneuvering around the stopped taxi, the people, and the occasional monkey, with far more speed and assurance than I would have been able to manage.

"Hurry, hurry!" pressed the first man. His beige kurta hung to his thighs and a red scarf was knotted at his neck.

Michael walked around the car to the front door and got in, while Aidan, Kellen, and I began to clamber in the back. We were still climbing in when the cab started to roll.

Only by focusing clearly on an object and stilling your mind can the higher Self, the purusa, be realized. Think of a lake. Most often the mind generates waves of thought, *vrtti*, that impede our ability to see deeply into the water. The surface roils and churns. When the mind is stilled, the waves settle, and the depths of the soul are revealed. Without such focus, the quieting of the waves, the busy mind fixates on everything else in the world, prakrti, and mistakes these objects—everything from a new car to your new child—as something permanent, abiding, or pure. It confuses the manifest for the unmanifest.

The fixation of the mind on the breath or a mantra, though, is not enough, Patanjali continues. Liberation doesn't happen if one just every now and then finds stillness. Our one-pointed focus must be done without interruption. How long remains unclear. The sutras assure us that liberation can happen within a lifetime, but they also prepare us to work through many cycles of birth and death. Most importantly, Patanjali insists that the one-pointedness must be done with devotion as well.

Most westerners remain unaware of the fact that yoga is essentially theistic. The practice of yoga in the United States—all asana with very little attention to the spiritual—only encourages the secularization of this four-thousand-year-old philosophy. But yoga centers on the Divine, and Patanjali's sutras become more emphatic on this point as you move deeper into the text. By the middle of the book, Patanjali clarifies that the best, quickest, and safest path to self-realization requires one-pointed focus on Isvara, God, alone. "If one lacks faith in Isvara, [enlightenment] remains remote, but if one's yoga is permeated with the nectar of devotion, it is very near." No wiggle room exists in the sutras. To free the purusa from the prakrti that binds it, you must devote yourself entirely to the Divine. "Surrender to God," the commentaries read, "is not an option." It is a mandatory part of the practice.

Several weeks ago, I was running in temperatures a few degrees below zero; a thick fog had rolled into the valley overnight from the north, concealing the sky above and the road ahead. My headlamp reflected light back into my eyes, the fog a wall of white. My route takes me into a depression, an area of low-lying fields and few houses. The road descends steeply enough that I can feel the temperature drop as I move down the hill. In the summer, I welcome the cool. In the winter, I dread it.

Given the starless sky and thick fog, the air felt close and pressing. High beams of trucks and cars would erupt out of nowhere, not twenty feet from me, to steal what little vision I had. Soon, not even headlights broke the fog. I could not see sky, mountain, or house. I ran blind.

At the very bottom of the hill, near the fields that lay empty in the winter, the fog consumed the sound as well. No longer able to hear my footfalls, I ran on air itself. Without sight, smell, sound, without senses, the world around me collapsed into the present moment. This stride. This stride. This stride. Nothing before or behind me. No way to gauge where I was in time or space. All just right now.

At that moment, a giant bird swooped down from a roost I could not see. Explosion of sound and motion and body. Air alive and beating. The bird brushed across the plane of my shoulders, the *tsk* of wings against the nylon, the touch certain, firm, and then fleeting. Within seconds it landed on an irrigation wheel I could barely see on the side of the road.

An owl.

Into that moment pressed another: the owl that had lifted our cat into the air more than twelve years ago, took her high into the sky before dropping her long body to the ground. Four talon marks in her belly. Too much trouble or weight for the bird to bear.

Had I been considered prey by this owl? My long, lit body in reflective gear? Or had the owl only been taking my measure, touching me, letting me know he was there?

He perched on the irrigation wheel, talons to steel, dark shadow in cloud. My heart raced; the feel of his wings still vibrated against my skin.

And then Kellen started screaming. Sitting in the middle of the backseat, I looked over at him. At first I thought he was just scared that the cab had moved. But then he cried even louder, pure panic on his face. I realized the cab had rolled onto his ankle, pinning it to the road.

"You're on his foot!" I yelled. "Back up! Back up!"

I pushed Aidan out the far door and followed him into the street. "You have run over his foot!!" I yelled. "Back up!"

When I reached the other side of the taxi, I could see the black tire pressing on Kellen's shoe. I didn't know if the car should move forward or backward. I also didn't know if the driver understood the problem.

Michael scrambled from the front seat and threw the pizza box to the ground as well as the groceries we had purchased earlier. Green mangoes wobbled down the hill, followed by a roll of toilet paper.

Aidan stood behind both of us, silent and white.

"What do we do?!" I called to Michael, but just then the taxi lurched backward, freeing Kellen's foot. Michael pulled him into his arms. Even though he was out of danger, I kept yelling. "You ran over his goddamned foot!" I pressed my hand to Kellen's hair and kept repeating: "His foot! His foot!"

A voice in my head reminded me that people don't really yell in India, at least not like that, and they certainly don't shout profanity in public, but I didn't care. I would be the strange American, the loud one. So I screamed for Kellen and the taxi driver who failed to look. I screamed to the crowds of people gathering and the host of monkeys in the trees. I also screamed for the helplessness I had felt since arriving in India, my inability to carry the poverty that surrounded me. I screamed to the sky for my ignorance, my fortune, my apathy.

The crowd thickened around us, several layers deep, voices offering all sorts of advice, in English, in Hindi. We had seen this kind of swarming around an accident before. When two cars ran into each other in a tiny mountain town, we had watched the people gather to comment, help, and chide.

A man, maybe the one who had led us to the taxi—I could not tell from all the hands reaching toward me—kept trying to take Kellen's shoe off. But I batted his hand away.

"Hospital? Hospital?" people offered.

"Jennifer, take his shoe off," Michael said. He held Kellen, who no longer wailed. Instead, he buried his face in Michael's shoulder, wishing, I imagined, to be home.

"Does your foot hurt when I try and take off your shoe?" I asked him. His head shook back and forth, so I gently worked the shoe, then the sock free.

The skin around his ankle throbbed angry red, the flesh raked but not broken open. Blood welled to the surface, tiny drops in rows running from lower shin to heel. He could, though, flex his foot and wiggle his toes. It didn't appear broken.

Taking Kellen from Michael, I held him to my body. He clung to my neck but said nothing. "You must have been so scared, Kellen. I'm so sorry. I'm so sorry. You must have been so scared."

I could feel his body shake.

Adrenaline pumped through my own body. I too was trembling. I tried to make out specific faces in the crowd, but I felt like a spectacle. I didn't want anyone's help. I didn't want to see individuals. I just wanted to be gone from there.

"Do you want to take a taxi home or do you want me to carry you?" I asked Kellen.

"Carry me," he said.

So I lifted my eight-year-old son and began to climb the hill.

In Patanjali's yoga I appreciate most his insistence that the things of the world, made of prakrti, are not illusion (*maya*). Taxis and monkeys and pizza boxes are not to be seen as ancillary or unimportant in the pursuit of the eternal. Plenty of other spiritual traditions encourage their followers to reject this earth, this existence, in favor of a better one in the future, the one that waits after death. I think of my gay Mormon students who are told to tread water during this lifetime because they will receive a new body, a heterosexual body, in the next. Instead, Patanjali suggests, prakrti exists to give us opportunities to liberate the soul. Practice is how I think about it. Every object, every thought, every relationship, every moment of our day provides us with the chance to see the possibility of the Divine. The world shows us how to learn to love.

But here is where I also part ways with Patanjali. For although he sees the purpose of prakrti in providing experiences in which we can discriminate the unmanifest (the Divine) from the manifest (everything else), he does not see the manifest as divine on its own. Prakrti, for Patanjali, might be useful, but it is not holy.

And I have been touched by an owl.

We made our way up the mountain, Michael and Aidan burdened with the groceries we had bought, me carrying Kellen on my back. Cars and motorcycles whipped past. Trucks pushed us to the narrow dirt margin. I kept asking Kellen if he was fine.

"It's okay, Mom," he reassured me, mouth against my ear. "It hurts like a bad scrape."

Halfway home, we passed a young cow with only three legs. A birth defect perhaps. The calf hobbled between the rocks and the tufts of withered grass. His brown eyes seemed too large for his small face, and his missing leg caused his body to lean at an angle against the mountain.

"We have to do something for him," Aidan said.

I slid Kellen from my back to a low rock wall and waited for Michael to reach us. Sweat ran down my face and arms even though clouds still hid the sun. Michael arrived, laden with everything but Kellen, and the four of us considered the calf who did not shy away at our approach.

"What's left of the groceries?" I asked Michael.

He looked into the newspaper-wrapped balls and pulled out a head of cauliflower.

We halved it and offered it to the cow, grateful for something to give.

When I picked Kellen back up and returned to the mountain climb, I realized that much of my anger had left me. I was still worried that we might have to take Kellen to a hospital, that some tiny foot bones had been fractured, but his injury could have been much worse. Maybe it was the effort required to keep moving up the hill, or the press of Kellen's body to my back, or the cow on the side of the road who walked the flank of a mountain on three legs, but I felt far away from the woman who had screamed obscenities to the sky, the one who sought some kind of crazy justice, the one who refused to accept the world as offered.

On that Friday morning, at the end of a week in which five students had cried in my office and the inmates had crumpled under fluorescent lighting and night after night I had watched the hours march forward from 1 a.m. to 2 a.m. to 3 a.m. as I worried, regretted, and planned, I closed my eyes and returned to my breath. I am breathing in, I said to myself. I am breathing out. Winter dark soaked the living room, three candles the only light. In my lap I held nothing, or I held everything, my students, the inmates, Kellen's foot pinned beneath a tire.

I am breathing in.

I am breathing out.

Nothing moved in the house. Not the cats or the boys asleep down the hall. Not the spruce outside the picture window.

In the now, the atha, the story I told about my students, myself, my son, fell away. The now contains no beginning, no middle, no end. It searches not into the future, nor does it cling to the past. I sat without seeing, hearing, or touching and awaited the glance of owl. Shiva stood in front of me, candle lit below. Though my eyes remained closed, I knew light danced on all his arms.

Here is the thing about the taxi in India. For two years I carried the story as one of harm or near miss. I pointed to that moment in our travels as a place where disaster was averted or anger justified or a man failed to look.

But the other day I realized that that moment on the mountain marks the last moment I carried my son. It records the end of an eight-year period that began with his birth, years in which I held him in my arms, first because he could not walk, later because I wanted to move more quickly than his toddler legs would go, and still later when he sought solace after a fall or a failure. Yes, Kellen still climbs into my lap sometimes or will snuggle with me on the couch when we read, but he weighs too much for me to actually pick up. I cannot physically bear him any longer.

I do not know the day I last carried Aidan. It has faded into the past, unmarked. But the taxi in India has given me that moment with Kellen. The brush with harm fastened my attention to his breath in my ear, the press of his body to my back, his weight, heavy but certain.

Now, Patanjali tells us, is the time for yoga. And how rarely do we actually practice? Look to the objects of the world as a place to see the Divine, he insists, and we close our eyes. The owl skims my shoulder blades. Kellen breathes in my ear. The calf eats our cauliflower, and a student hands me *not* her suffering but a stone from a path of healing she has hewn on her own. The manifest and the unmanifest are not joined but the same. Now is the time.

The Wanting Creature

We left for the Dalai Lama's temple a little after six in the morning. Clouds snagged the tops of the Himalayas, still snow covered even in June. In the plum trees, bulbuls sounded their alarms, long cries that woke us each morning just as the skies began to lighten, and did not cease until nightfall. Aidan and Kellen greeted the cow tethered in the neighbor's yard as well as the random stray dogs they had named and now loved. I helped them tally the number of banana slugs we found to keep their minds off the earliness of the hour and the steepness of the slope. My parents had just recently joined us in India, a little over a month into our three-month stay. They shook their heads each time we climbed the grassy hill to the road where we would then face a longer and steeper ascent to town.

"Is up the only option?" they joked.

We joined the maroon-robed monks who walked the pilgrim's trail singly and in pairs. Pilgrims, many of them wearing traditional Tibetan clothes, accompanied them. All carried mala beads in their hands, most of them chanting just above a whisper. *Om mani padme hum*. Prayer flags dressed the pines in color.

"The monks must have cleared the forests of monkeys for His Holiness's presence," I said to Michael and smiled. We didn't see a single macaque. Even the cows had remained home, which left the woods to the crows and the supplicants.

As we drew closer to the temple complex, the prayer wheels appeared. Over three hundred line the path. We spun every one, chanting as we moved up the hill, acknowledging the Divine in everything. The wooden handles were smoothed and softened by the thousands of hands that had touched them before. The wheels spun easily. Bright bell. Green cedars. Another prayer.

At the martyr's plaza, Tibetans chanted with monks in long rows on the ground. Their words trailed the incense, sweet and thick, that lifted into the morning sky. We walked past the pictures of the martyrs, the young monks who self-immolated in protest of China's occupation of Tibet. It would have been easier to keep my head down, to avoid the wall of photos altogether, but I slowed, looked at each of the fifty or so faces—most of them smiling, some of them already aflame. The chants reverberated in my chest, all those low murmurs, the quiet urgency, something stirring deep and strong.

We gave money every time we walked to town. Gave money to the sadhus who sat in the woods in their orange robes and cooked meals from a single pot, gave to the thin man scarred from flame, gave to the old woman who had lost much of her face to leprosy and who cupped the coins in blood-bandaged hands, gave to the children who reached out from their mothers' arms, gave to the bent men who pulled themselves up the hill on wooden blocks or wheeled planks, gave to anyone and everyone who asked. Such actions, though, seemed flimsy at best. A coin here. A coin there. In the face of all that suffering, I was realizing that your presence, your ability to be present, mattered more. Moving toward, rather than away. Taking those bandaged hands in your own, carrying the backpack for the man with no legs, smiling at the woman who begs for her children. With that in mind, I looked into the eyes of the martyrs, wished them freedom from suffering, tried to be fully there.

That focus though, that presence, vanished as soon as we turned the corner at the top of the hill and arrived at the gate leading to the Dalai Lama's temple. A line of hundreds stretched down the street, filled with Westerners, most of them young, who stood in clumps and shifted from leg to leg eating bananas and drinking chai and laughing under the sun. We weren't the only ones hoping to see the Dalai Lama. Every few minutes, the line moved forward, but mostly we stood.

"We should have left earlier," I complained to Michael. "Or taken the road instead of the pilgrim's path. We could have done the prayer wheels another day."

"It will be okay," he responded and returned to the hand games he was playing with the boys. I simmered in silence and counted the number of people in front of us.

Nearby, a couple was buying thin white cloths from a woman at a stall. The woman demonstrated for the couple how to hold the scarf, across your hands like an offering. After they left, I went over and asked what the white scarves were for.

"For His Holiness to bless."

"How much are they?"

"Twenty rupees."

Two minutes later, we had six scarves. I knew, given the line, that there would be hundreds of people in the audience. I envisioned, as I stood outside the temple, that His Holiness would give a kind of "global blessing," and we would all hold up our scarves. The blessing would filter through the air, lodge in the fibers, and we could hang the white cloth on our walls at home, point to it when guests came over.

"Excuse me," a woman, possibly French, asked, "Do you think we will be close enough to His Holiness to receive a blessing?"

"I just saw someone else buying the scarves, so we bought them," I shrugged.

"Better to be safe," she said.

I realized then that for the blessing to "count," we would have to move close enough to have His Holiness actually touch it. Silently, I considered our relative position in line.

Maybe an hour or so later, we made it through security and were released into the central courtyard. It felt good to be out of line, like we were making progress. The courtyard was a large square area shaded by white tents and tall, leafy trees. Even though I had been expecting chairs instead of ground, there did seem to be space for everyone to sit. People dropped to the grass or to stone slabs. Many leaned against the railings.

We took places near the front, not far from where it looked like His Holiness would speak. Because we had arrived relatively early and because the courtyard was so large, we easily found places close to what appeared to be a stage. We sat on a low stone wall and waited.

A woman nearby turned to us.

"If you can find a place on the railing, His Holiness will probably bless your boys. He loves children."

I immediately scoped out the railing, looking for empty space. Behind us, people entered the courtyard by the scores, having made it through security. Within minutes, every low wall had been taken, every patch of grass was gone.

I saw a space still free on the railing, close to the home of His Holiness. I took the boys, and we wedged ourselves between the other Westerners. Michael and my parents remained where they had been. Soon I lost sight of them in the crowds.

"Okay," I said to Aidan and Kellen, "be ready for when he comes out. You'll want to lean over with your scarves, really stretch."

The boys practiced. I made sure to keep claiming enough space along the railing, wide legged and solid.

A group of young monks, monks not much older than my sons, arrived in a group and stood below us.

"How can I reach over them," Kellen wailed. "I can't reach."

I tried not to be angry at the monks. They were monks after all, and young, but they had jeopardized my plan. Then it occurred to me that maybe we could use the monks. Surely the Dalai Lama would want to come over and bless these young men in service to the Buddha. Maybe we could leverage their position.

"I'll boost you up," I said to Kellen.

"I'll never reach," he cried.

"Well, it'll be okay if he doesn't actually bless your scarf. He has a lot of people to see."

"No," he asserted, "it won't. He has to bless it. That's the whole point."

Half an hour later, I was still at work holding our space on the rail. I had to fight off a Tibetan woman and then a young man who didn't speak English. I stared at the gates to the Dalai Lama's home, willing him to come out before we lost our good position. While I was at it, I willed him to move to his right first. Surely he will move to the right. I glanced about for the hundredth time, trying to determine if there was a better place and feeling bitterness at all those who took up too much room.

Suddenly, an announcement. "We need everyone to organize into groups based on nationalities," the voice said. "His Holiness will take a picture with each group. If you are from South America, you need to be over here. Central America over here."

I lost the rest of what he was saying with the realization that all my maneuvering at the railing was for naught. All that standing, guarding, practicing, all that guessing, willing, plotting, in vain. I gave up my claim on the rail, watched the monks leave for their appointed place.

The Americans made their way over to their section of the courtyard—more Americans, by far, than we had seen since leaving the United States. People started forming a line where it appeared His Holiness might walk through.

"Quick," I said to Aidan, pushing him forward. "Get up there!"

The boys stood at the front, but just as quickly a guard came by and told us to move to a different area. With each new space, I pushed and pulled the boys to the front.

"Here," I said. "You can hold your scarf this way."

"Here," I said. "He will surely see you."

After four hours, that would be four hours after we set out from our home, His Holiness walked through the gates. By then, I was exhausted. The panic I had carried for the last several hours—how will I get them close to the Dalai Lama—had worn me down. I sat on the ground, ready to go home.

Before coming to India, I had not specifically wanted to see the Dalai Lama. Before hearing he was giving a public audience for foreigners, I had not wanted to listen to him talk. Before learning about the white scarves, I hadn't wanted to own one. Before realizing the possibility of a blessing, I hadn't needed one. Yet, there I was, in a crowd of Buddhists no less, angling for the best space. Planning, devising, pushing, needing, wanting. Worse, I had made the boys want the same thing.

"I'll never have a blessing," Kellen cried at one point, somewhere deep into four hours of waiting. He had left without breakfast. We hadn't taken water. There were no chairs.

"Yes, you will," I insisted.

Michael, though, picked him up. "He has already blessed us Kellen. He already has."

Poppycock, I thought. I want that blessed scarf.

My entire morning with the Dalai Lama was spent wanting. Things I hadn't known existed at six in the morning suddenly became centrally important by noon. And I gave so much energy to that wanting—allowed it to determine my experience at the temple. I didn't hear a word of his talk. Didn't interact with the people around me. Couldn't tell you the kinds of trees that grew in the courtyard.

As it turned out, the boys were at the front and center of the picture with the Dalai Lama. His Holiness touched both of them. Through no effort of my own, they stood next to him. I, on the other hand, wasn't even in the picture. Which I find perfect, since I was never fully at the temple.

The following morning, I thought about my derailed visit as I ran up through town and then along a mountain road. Between the cedars and pines, I caught glimpses of the Himalayan peaks. The morning sun tossed crowns of light into the sky, and the snow shone bright like glass. In India I ran early, before the vendors opened for the day, before the streets became clogged with people, cars, and dogs. And that morning only my wanting creature accompanied me in the woods.

My thoughts turned to home, to northern Utah in June, when the yellow mule's ears carpet the mountains and the hillsides are green and bright. I love living in the tiny town of Logan for so many reasons. The mountains, the rivers, the canopy of sky. But that morning I thought mostly about all that Logan didn't have: a Banana Republic, a Target, an Apple Store. Instead, we had Old Navy. That was it. Such lack of retail options kept my wanting creature in check. I didn't want because there was nothing to want. Like an alcoholic who never brings alcohol into the house, I was fine as long as I never opened a catalog. But my wanting creature only bided his time, waited.

In India my privilege was so easy to see. I only needed to leave the house and my gross good fortune became clear. Too often, though, I measured my wealth materially—I had a good job, a retirement, a house, two cars—while those on the streets had much less. My own lack hadn't occurred to me amid all that poverty. I realized as I ran that morning that the trick was not in remaining present in the face of others' needs. It was remaining present in the face of my own wanting.

As I came down the mountain from my run, I noticed that a group had formed outside the entrance to the Dalai Lama's temple. Since it was only six in the morning, few had gathered. At first I thought His Holiness must be giving a second audience. As I got closer, though, I realized the people weren't queued as much as clustered.

"What's happening?" I asked a Tibetan woman.

"His Holiness is about to depart."

I found a place along the street and sat down to wait. I wondered what "about" might mean. Four hours? How would I let Michael know that I was sitting on the roadside waiting for the Dalai Lama? Memories of the day before washed over me, feelings of frustration, emptiness, and loss. I didn't want to derail another morning. And then I wondered if I even needed to sit there. If I wanted to sit there. And why I might remain.

Above me, the trees waved against the sky. Another beautiful day. Monkeys jumped from limb to limb. Near me, two men unfolded their white scarves, holding them as offerings across their hands. I thought of Michael and the boys waiting for me at home; of the man with no legs who greeted me every morning with a wide smile, his hands folded to his chest; of the morning sun on the snow. I realized it was really fine if I missed the Dalai Lama. My day would still be full. I could simply walk back home.

I started to rise, to leave, when the police cars drove past, lights flashing. Then several dark sedans, monks sitting in the backseats with their hands folded in their laps. Then the car with the Dalai Lama.

We all bowed at the waist, hands in prayer; some of the women prostrated themselves on the ground. His car neared me, and I looked up into his eyes as he passed. He smiled. Maybe at me, maybe at the woman next to me, maybe at a shadow in the glass. Regardless, the grace went straight to my heart. I felt its warmth lodge in my chest. There on the streets, still in my running clothes, sweat drying on my skin, arms brushing against the woman next to me, I wasn't given anything I didn't already have.

Lobster

You are eleven, and when you push the locks down on the van doors, it is with a child's certitude. Your thumb presses the dimple in the plastic, pushes the head down, and the finality of the action soothes, a lid atop a boiling pot, a bedroom door shut to the mess, a penis returned to shorts.

"Don't look at him," you yell to your younger brothers, the ones your parents charged you with watching before they entered the deep. "Get down."

But they don't listen, faces and palms pressed to the windows of the sliding van door. Instead they watch the man who sits on the log; they wait to see what he will do.

At least you are in the van.

The van sits in the sandy parking lot, some thirty yards from a beach without a name. Hou Beach, your father calls it, for the trees that thread and track just above the sand line—branches running horizontal, limber and bent, full green leaves emerging from the ends, a jungle gym you can walk on, have walked on, just today in fact, earlier, before your parents boarded the Zodiac, masked and suited. On a narrow inlet on the windward side of Oahu, Hou Beach boasts a crescent of sandy shore, a concrete bathroom with doorless stalls, a water spigot, and shade. Empty now, save for the dive gear that litters the beach, the fins and snorkels left—abandoned—before the divers set out, hours ago.

Well, not empty. You see a few members of the dive club cleaning their gear at the faucet—fresh water rinsing sand from flippers, snorkels, the metal clasps—don't forget the metal—it rusts—salt water—corrodes the shine to brown—scabbed—use your fingers—scrub—only vigilance will keep the chrome shiny. The remaining dive club members lay the gear in the sun to dry; the man sitting on the log pulls his penis from his shorts.

"Gross!!" Scott cries. "He's peeing!"

But he isn't peeing, this man, browned in the sun, wearing no shirt, neither young nor old, three feet from the van; he is masturbating. You want not to know this.

"No, he's not," you insist. "He's—just get down."

The man looks up at the three of you—you in the passenger seat looking out, door locked, thumb to dimple, click, and your brothers, ages five and eight, in the back seat, silent again—and his mouth turns into an "o" that is both grin and grimace. His eyes meet yours.

They are looking for "bug." Hou Beach is famous for them. Lobster, the kind that live in the Pacific—not the ones with giant claws, one bigger than the other, smooth red-and-green shell, the ones you see in the comics, but the buggier kind—slipper lobster, two long antennae, eyes, and a curled tail that tucks under their bodies in shame. Known to be the best at spotting bug, your father's eyes can read a reef like a contract, can see shells and octopi and lobster when others just keep pointing to the colorful fish. His world does not dissemble. A military lawyer, he moves past all the lies, reaches into the hole of truth and pulls out the bug. He and your mom took goody bags the size of your body with them on the boat. As the man not-pees beside you—whites of eyes, hands thrusting—your parents skim the bottom of the sea, shed weights to conserve air, watch for the thick black antennae that give the lobster away, glove their hands against the spines and reach into the dark.

"What do we do?" Scott asks.

He is no longer laughing, maybe because the man is not moving, now just sits and stares at the three of you. You thought you were looking at him, but now you realize you are the one being watched.

"Just keep the doors locked," you respond with a kind of learned authority you don't feel. Searching the blue-and-white vw van for a weapon, you see sand on the floor mats and a straw. Your parents will emerge from the sea within the next few hours. The air begins to feel close and thick, sun slanting through windows, sweat slicking the pale white skin of your armpits.

Your father's friend doesn't keep his penis in his shorts. When he comes to visit, he sits on the webbed chairs on the lanai and drinks bourbon slushes while his dick lolls next to his leg, a log. He must know his penis is exposed. Temperature alone would seem to be enough, like when you stick your leg outside the sheet at night, cool air riddling the hairs on your shin. You think of the man's penis as a dog, the man's friend, his pet. When you sit across from the man, slurping your virgin bourbon slush, hands sticky with orange juice, ice melting in the Hawaiian sun, you try to look anywhere but at the dog. The dog lolls and pants, jiggles with every shift. You realize you are not looking away.

The man outside the van is sticky as well, his hands. He presses his thumb and finger together, tacky, and holds them up for you to examine. Inside the van, the three of you shriek; he smiles, slow, nose wrinkled. Then he returns to his penis, again. You consider honking the horn, maybe to scare him away or draw attention to the van, to the three of you trapped inside, but you don't know if the car has to be on for the horn to work. Your parents did not leave you the keys—why would they, you don't drive, you are barely old enough to have a military ID card—but did they take the keys with them into the sea? All that metal? What about rust?

They did take their knives, barbed and angry and strapped to their shins. Your father's blade is longer and thicker than your mother's. The point is certain, not a fleck of rust on the steel. If they see a shark, they will take their knives and bang their air tanks to alert others. Clang, clang. If they see an eel, they will press their first two fingers and thumb together again and again: eel. If they are low on air, they will cut their hands across their necks and head for the surface. Your parents have an entire language they use under the sea, a vocabulary of distress.

There is no sign for a man with a penis on a log.

They will return. At some point. They always do. A ring circles your mother's face, red and welted, from where the mask fits too close. Water drips from earlobes, flippers in hand. They will walk up the beach, black clad and sleek, and drop their gear in the grass. You will have also returned, from the van not the sea, and you will run to greet them.

"What did you get? What did you get?"

They will offer their goody bags, and you will plunder the spoil: cowries, marbled cones, beach glass sanded to softness. The lobster will thump and rattle in a separate, larger mesh bag, slowly dying in the sun. At home, your mother will contain them in the stainless-steel sink in the kitchen. Meekly they will try to climb atop one another to escape, but against the steep sides, they only fall back on themselves. That night a large pot of boiling water will fill the kitchen with steam, and your mother will don gloves once again and place each struggling lobster into the roiling bath.

Two will fit in the pot, and she will quickly slam the lid down to keep both lobster and steam from escaping. A shrill whistle will sound through the house as the lobster die; it will careen from the lidded pot and scream from the kitchen, and it will find you in your bedroom, where you sit balled on your bed, pillow over your head, and it will dive deep into your ears.

Incantation

My father's mood could be registered in song. From my bedroom as a child, I kept my head lifted from pillow and hair pulled away in order to hear. A day that began with music meant one that might not end in anger. His voice was not great, but he knew that. Like mine, the tune he heard in his head was probably more elastic and sonorous than the one he produced. Still, he loved to sing, whether hymns from his childhood, the Everly brothers, Elvis Presley, Simon and Garfunkel, or even the occasional Janis Joplin, anything that had a steady beat with lyrics suggesting triumph rather than despair. Not every day, not even every other, but often, while driving to the beach or bending over his workbench, my father broke into song.

I imagine there wasn't much music in his house growing up. I know of no stories where he and his brothers gathered by the radio at night, no music lessons, no church choirs. The Brownie camera movies I have seen of family gatherings show my father chasing his cousins around long picnic tables filled with bowls of salad but no guitars. Yet, family lore posits a picture of my twenty-year-old mother, sitting at a piano in my grandparents' living room on her first visit to their house, surrounded by my father and his sister and brothers with their wives, all leaning in like a forest. They feed on my mother's fingers as she flies up and down the keys, holding her captive carol after carol until the Nebraska sky grows as black as the soil deep beneath their feet.

An overhead lamp illuminates her face and casts the rest of her body in shadow.

"Heart of my heart," my father sings from the kitchen, whisking the eggs before he scrambles them, "I love that melody." To the softly bubbling eggs he will add chopped celery and handfuls of grated cheese. Several rooms away, I imagine him turning with my mother, his hands along her waist, guiding her around the table as if they are in a dance hall rather than a dining room. While I have only watched them jitterbug together and never waltz, especially around the dining room where the chairs stand close to the wall and make dancing impossible, I hold onto the idea that my mother resides in his heart of hearts and that he sings for her. And I learn to love that melody.

That is it, though. All that I have of that song. Heart of my heart, I love that melody. Eight words over and over again, sometimes accompanied by a Crosby-like croon, ba, ba, ba, boom, but mostly just those eight words. In fact, almost every song my father sang was a ghost of itself. "Rock of ages cleft for me." That's all. "Mariah, Mariah, they call the wind Mariah." No more. "Thunder, thunder, thunder was his name." Nothing else. I used to wonder if there were more words to the songs my father sang, wondered if maybe he was too deeply involved in whatever he was doing to bother with the verses or even manage the complete refrain. But over time the bits of song, sung so often, grew whole in themselves, so I learned not to focus on what came next or even care. The eight words, or six, or four, were the ones that mattered, the central ones, the only ones worth holding onto.

Because my father either couldn't or didn't want to remember the lyrics to most of the songs he sang, he made them up. Anything would do. Driving to the beach, he would use the surroundings and the occupants of the car as material. Suddenly, he would begin "Oh Dear What Can the Matter Be," and you were stuck in the lavatory with seven old ladies and could only hope you would be the first to be sprung. On these days, we played a favorite game that entailed choosing a word for a person who would then have to make up a song using the word. My brothers and I always gave my father the word "orange" because we had heard it was the only word in English that didn't have a rhyme. Such limitations didn't stop my father, who could spin a song about fruit before we had made it out of the driveway. Nothing delighted him more than making the rhyme seem easy and apparent. It was much harder for me. My mind couldn't think quickly enough to choose a reasonable ending word so that I would have an easy time finding a rhyming one. My songs fell to the ground in a heap, having crashed at the end of the line.

That my father has bequeathed me a legacy of songs that dead-end after a few words could be seen as a source of frustration. After all, when all you know of the song is "Thunder, thunder, thunder was his name," you feel a bit frenetic as you sing. You don't arrive anywhere. Because I never knew the "he" named Thunder, as a child I imagined a man pounding ties for the railroad, a man whose hammer blows were as mighty as claps overhead. Perhaps my father sang more of that song to me, and I am the one who has amputated it so mercilessly. Perhaps it really was about the railroad, and I have forgotten. I could easily find out. Check the internet, ask my father, spend some time with the songbooks from my childhood. Instead, as I did as a child, I would rather leave the lyrics brief and recursive, like an incantation that conjures my father, the past, and moments when the only difficulty was finding an end rhyme.

If my father's songs were amputated, my mother's mother's would not end. Having never quite recovered from the fact that she would spend her life in South Dakota and not on the stage, my grandmother wore refinement like a sidearm. On plane trips to see us in Hawaii, she dressed in skirts that flirted with her knees, heels in every shade of purple, and an ermine stole that chased its tail around her neck. Before her suitcase was set down in the house, my father had a drink ready for her, the ice nervously clattering against an already damp glass. Even when her plane arrived in the morning.

Everything about her was severe, the way she pulled her hair away from her face, the line where her eye shadow ended, her tolerance for noise. She spoke in complete sentences, handed out French expressions as if they were mints, and smoked Pall Malls by the carton. In a family where we ate casseroles still wearing our play clothes and fought over what cereal to open next, my grandmother spent her time with us on the edge of her chair, waiting to flee. Where she wished to run, I imagine, was to the past, the years during the war when soldiers hungered for the company of beautiful women and dancing with men was a wartime duty. Even though she was married to my grandfather and had my infant mother to care for at home, what sustained her in the sleepy towns of South Dakota were the dances held for the soldiers home on leave, dances where men spun her twenty-two-inch waist while her silk scarf fluttered like a flag. Late at night, after the baby was in bed, she would slip out to the dance hall, a building aflame against the Black Hills. In fact, the night my grandfather came home from the war, it was to an empty house. He set down his duffel bag, lit a cigarette, and waited in the living room for his young wife to return. When she entered the room sometime after midnight, he thought he was being visited by an angel, having forgotten just how beautiful she was. Years later, he would be the one to fly away.

By the time I knew her, she was deeply unhappy. Nothing could measure up to those moments of freedom in the early forties, the big band music, the late nights, the headiness of war. An unfaithful husband, a heart attack, the bottle, and the loss of her house to a flood left her bitter and angry. Which is why,

I think, she sought refuge in art, both painting and music, as a way to imagine other possibilities, other endings, to a life that had held so much promise.

She made up for the lack of brightness in her life with oil canvasses layered in slabs of electric color. Her paintings had texture and charge, even though her subjects—landscapes—were mild and literal. Palm trees quivered in limes and chartreuses, their trunks bending toward the horizon. Mountains literally lifted from the canvas in painterly brush strokes that suggested flight. The twenty-year-old girl who yearned to dance professionally appeared in every bush and stump.

Because of the noise and distractions in our house, she never painted in front of me but waited until she returned home. I only saw the pieces years later, long after she was dead, a diary in acrylics. Her paintings complicate her life, insist that I see the woman holding the brush differently, that I pay attention to the language of color. Her palette and stroke suggest an artist who felt imprisonment in everything she saw. As a child, though, I had trouble seeing past the grim expression and wrinkled skin, the costume jewelry, the hair pieces, the eyebrows tweezed into submission.

Her love of music did little to change my opinion. When we visited my grandmother in Rapid City, she would play her organ for us, an instrument that produced, to my ears, the muddiest of sounds. The notes clung to me like sand at the shore and would not let go. I hated to listen to her play, hated the way I couldn't tell where one sound ended and another began, hated the breathiness and constant swelling of notes. She would offer me the bench when she was finished, and I would pump the foot pedal feverishly to achieve the strongest sound, only to have it fade as quickly as it was played. Nothing held. My brother Scott and I would flip the stops up and down, adding trumpets and violas, marimbas and bass, trying to a find a series that pleased. Within ten minutes, we were sent outside to play in her tiny backyard mined with dog poop.

When she visited us, things were better, if only because the Hawaiian weather meant my brothers and I could be outdoors. My mother would sit at our piano, an upright baby grand that her parents bought as a wedding present, and play, while my grandmother stood beside her, one hand resting on the piano and the other on her diaphragm, singing like a diva. Songs that I would have recognized if my mother had been singing—"Mr. Bojangles" or "Somewhere over the Rainbow"—seemed to sprout new limbs in my grandmother's mouth, trilling and spilling and melting into one gigantic "o" of a sound, not unlike the organ. Up and down the register, she vibratoed while my mother watched for signals to pause, to turn, to begin again. Their concentration turned our family room into a performance hall; I whispered in between numbers. My legs would grow tired of standing and waiting for the song to end so that I could ask for a snack or a ride to soccer practice.

Or maybe it was jealousy that caused my impatience, made me sigh at the edge of the room or whine about hunger, and here, perhaps, is why my grandmother and her music matter to me now, why I find myself writing about moments long forgotten. My mother and grandmother were enjoying themselves. I could tell by the way they caught each other's eyes and scurried through the sheet music debating about which song to perform next. They also needed each other to make their music. Though I took piano lessons, I found no joy in it. My mother forced me to practice twenty minutes a day, and I spent most of that time concocting stories for my piano teacher to justify my lack of progress. No easy grace emerged from my movements, no fluidity. And I was always alone at the keys. Leaning in the doorway, listening to lyrics I could not understand, I envied the shared repertoire, the history of music, their heads bent to touching over a song. At the age of nine or ten, I could not imagine myself being with my mother in such a meaningful way. Nor did it appear I would ever be as accomplished. The ability to play, paint, sew, sing, cook, and dance came to a grinding halt in my body.

Music took my mother away from me. When she sat down to play Grieg or Chopin before dinner, I knew not to bother her, not because she told me but because the music cast a spell around her, a castle made of notes. Unlike my father and I, who could not carry a tune, my mother's voice was clear and perfectly pitched. We would stumble for the lyrics and the melody to "Frankie and Johnny," while she would lead us home, feeding us the words and tune, never forgetting a verse.

She never sang while she worked. My mother was not one to hum while doing the dishes or folding the clothes. She might have music playing on the reel-to-reel, but she would only listen. When she sang, she was centered on singing. Her voice was an event, not a sound in the background. Some nights we would sit in the living room, my father with his ukulele and my mother with our songbook, and we would go through the songs one at a time. "Dead Skunk in the Middle of the Road," "Hang Down Your Head Tom Dooley," "When Johnny Comes Marching Home," "Proud Mary." The windows would grow bright with our reflections as the night came on, and we would remain at the coffee table, waiting for my mother to begin the next song.

When I was twelve, my mother joined the Julie Singers, a choir comprised of military wives who performed at shopping malls and holiday events around Honolulu. She accompanied the singers on the piano and lent her voice as well, wearing their navy-blue muumuu with a white Peter Pan collar and a floppy red bow. Many of their songs were military standards, but they also sang contemporary music like "Up with People" and "What

Color is God's Skin," songs that were new to me. My father and brothers and I would drive to the mall to watch them perform, pointing to my mother sitting at the piano, her back straight and hands poised above the keys, awaiting the nod of the conductor. As she played, she kept time with her entire being, becoming the beat, her foot pulsing on the pedals, her head nodding almost imperceptibly, her body moving in and away from the keyboard like the surf. In those moments, my mother was no longer my mother, the one who packed my lunch, did laundry on Tuesdays and Saturdays, and made me eat quenelles even though I hated fish. She occupied a different space, one I only later learned to recognize as her own. I was proud of her in her performance costume, loved to imagine I could pick her voice out from the other sopranos, and happy when she would practice the new pieces at home. She seemed a faraway star.

While music brought me closer to my father, bits of line repeated over and over, so that you swung from one to the next, it created division between me and my mother. Much like those moments at the piano with my grandmother, I felt abandoned each time my mother left the house in her muumuu. Because I could neither play nor sing, I saw no way to follow. I suppose all children want to own their parents, want their mother to never look away, but because we moved often as a military family, my fear of being left was tangible. I hated being away from my parents, from my mother in particular, and would cry every time they went out at night. The amputated songs of my father were familiar shards, not unlike the fragments of places we had lived, the general gist of a location, the refrain. As we did when we worked to "make weight" before we moved, he kept what he needed from a song and discarded the rest. My father also wasn't home much. Briefs or treaties or calls from the Philippines kept him on base for long days. When he was home, he was often angry at the broken vacuum cleaner or his inability to find a certain wrench or screwdriver. If he was found singing, then all was safe. But my mother was there every day we arrived home from school in every state in which we were ever stationed. Teachers, addresses, phone numbers, and bedrooms changed, but she remained. Music threatened all of that.

So I joined the Subase Chapel Children's Choir on Pearl Harbor Naval Station. One Sunday a month we would perform, entering the church wearing white robes made from sheets and turquoise blue stoles draped around our necks. "Let's go, let's go. Our junior marching song," we sang as we walked in line down the aisle. "Win one for Jesus," we continued. In front of a congregation comprised of submariners and their families, we would sing about Noah and Jonah, Cain and Abel, Esau and his hairy arms, often using hand motions like a show choir, shading our eyes when we took on the role of Zacchaeus looking out from the tree, wagging pretend lanterns at our sides when we sang about "this little light of mine."

I loved performing and looked forward to practice on Tuesdays. Even though anyone could join the choir, I felt special. The choir practiced in the evenings, after the sun had set and we had eaten dinner. I felt older than my ten years walking up the stairs to the chapel, entering the empty church, the stained-glass windows now dark. For the first few years, I went by myself, without Scott, who would join later, so the experience was all mine. I was also one of the oldest members, entering the chapel last on days we performed because of my height, taking my place in the back row.

We practiced in the balcony, hovering at the same level as the chandeliers. Each Tuesday, Mrs. G., the conductor, would tape a treat under one of the brown folding chairs. I wished every time for it to be mine. I loved hanging above the empty chapel, the windows below me, waiting to hear Mrs. G. sing our newest song. I loved the orderly way we walked into the church on Sundays, from shortest to tallest, singing the whole way. I loved how our robes concealed our regular clothes, transformed us into a choir. I would ask my mother to take us to church early and then hurry to sort through the stained and worn sheets looking for one that came down to my shins and was thick enough to hide the patterns in my dress. The days we performed were magical to me. I belonged.

Then came the spring of sixth grade, when I was asked to solo in our final concert of the season. Mrs. G. gave me a cassette tape of the song I was to sing, and I took it home and practiced diligently. As I never did with the piano, I went over and over the music. So much was at stake. Yes, an audience occupied by both of my parents, but more keenly the opportunity to share something I loved, something that had felt precious and special, something that made me feel larger than myself. And yet, I knew I couldn't sing. Years of being gently led back to the tune by my mother made me aware of my limitations. My voice cracked on any note above A, turning into a whisper as I stretched for the pitch. The song Mrs. G. had selected for me was about mud, and bugs, and God's love, and far too much of it reached above A. Hand motions and swinging hips would not ferry enough attention away from the fact that I could not find the notes. And at the age of twelve, I was no longer cute.

I stumbled through the performance, managing not to wince when my voice squeaked, all the time thinking of my mother, whose voice was as clear as water. I was pained to hear the soured notes, to know how short I had fallen. My parents made a tape of my solo, and I refused to listen to it. "In the sticky mud . . ." I can remember singing, my toes wiggling beneath my robe, my voice reaching and reaching and never arriving, "and catching a bug that glows."

At the end of the season I joined the bell choir.

For the next three decades I never sang in front of anyone, didn't even sing in the shower. I quit the piano. Never joined another choir. My performance in sixth grade seemed to affirm what I had always known: I could not sing like my mother. My father's fragments felt silly in my mouth. It was best to remain silent. Listen instead. And what I turned to were the records that lined the stereo cabinet shelves in the living room like so many soldiers. Records where words mattered. Lying on the carpet in front of the stereo, my brothers and I listened to an album called *Storytellers* again and again for entire afternoons. Songs like "Ruby, Don't Take Your Love to Town," "The Night the Lights Went Out in Georgia," "Cat's in the Cradle," and "The Gambler" spun tales of murder and deceit, humor and loss, but always with a beginning, middle, and end. Each verse complicated the story, drove the plot further, with the refrain giving us time to recover, to pause, to consider the central concern. And though I couldn't always make out the words—Don't trust a soul or no backwards son or lawyer?—I was never in doubt of the narrative arc. A cheating husband, an unfaithful wife, a man whose time had come. I wanted to be taken on the journey, wanted to move deeper into the sadness, have the songwriter help me understand how the world worked, have the singer show me pain. My youngest brother, Bryan, and I would be in tears by the end of "Seasons in the Sun," mourning a life cut short. We pitied the son who loses his father and then his son in "Cat's in the Cradle," vowing to never forget to play ball with our own children. We followed the songs like scripture.

The albums that inspired me as a child taught me the power of a well-told tale, the ability of a story to both seduce and distress a listener. Looking back now, I recognize that even though I have never considered myself a musician, much of what I know about writing comes from the music of my childhood. The narratives I eventually learned to write occupy a middle space between the fragments my father bequeathed with room enough to ramble and the thread-like ability of my mother's voice to bind the heart and ear. Though I could not sing, I could write, not songs but stories, and in those stories I eventually found the kind of freedom my grandmother experienced when she painted a palm, the space my lamp-lit mother occupied when playing Grieg, the spell that erased the anger from my father's eyes in only eight words.

I moved nine times in my first eighteen years but have only moved once in the past twenty, and that was a distance of thirty miles. I became a writer and teacher, as well as a mother of two boys. Words root me to my life; story gives me a line to follow, a way to mark my days, understand my life, know the stakes of my own tale. And I sing. It began when our sons were infants, and Michael and I would sing them to sleep. Aidan was a fussy baby who always wanted to be held. I walked him for miles around the house, singing whatever came into my head. At first, the standards: "Rockabye, Baby" or "Edelweiss." But soon my father's songs returned to me. "Proud Mary" and "Tom Dooley," "You Are My Sunshine" and "Amazing Grace." Sometimes entire verses would return, more often just a line. "Mariah, Mariah, they call the wind Mariah." I would sing my father into the darkening room as I paced back and forth with my crying son, the present joining the past and the future, ferried on the backs of seven words.

Fifteen years ago, my parents went backpacking in Patagonia. They were gone for many weeks, several of which were spent with other members of my extended family in Torres del Paine National Park. Patagonia blows cold and windy. At times, she said, my mother worried about the wind picking her up and taking her away, backpack and all. Even though it made the hiking harder, she carried extra gear to keep herself weighted to the earth. The winds never stopped. They raged during breakfast, followed them all day on the trail, and whaled their tents at night. While the scenery was remarkable, the trip sounded like hell to me.

My mother got a cold while she was in Patagonia, an ugly cold that pounded her head for days. She could not breathe, her ears refused to clear, and her nose ran constantly. Even after she returned to the States, she could not shake it.

Not one to take medicine and never one to go to the doctor, my mom left her body to fight the infection. Back in Dallas, she tried to go about her day working and grocery shopping, figuring out what to fix for dinner. But the cold would not leave. Finally, at my father's insistence, she went to the doctor. There she learned that the virus she had contracted in Patagonia, a microscopic bug, had eaten all the nerves in her right ear, had devoured her ability to hear. The loss happened within twenty-four hours of contracting the virus. She never had a chance. Nerves do not grow back. From that day forward, I would have to walk on her left side, worry about where to seat her at dinner, repeat my requests for her to pass the salad again and again. From that day forward, she would live a little less fully in the world.

My mother plays the piano rarely now. Maybe her work as a CASA volunteer or her quilting keep her too busy, but I wonder if it has to do with her ear. She also rarely sings. At least I haven't heard her. If you lose half of your hearing, do you lose half of your love for the heard? What would it mean to me if I lost half of my words? What story could I tell then? How would I compensate for all that was lost? Would I be like a two-year-old who chains nouns together with the occasional verb and waits for the listener to add the connectives? That my mother will never fully hear a symphony again creates a hole in my heart that no words can fill.

She is not alone in what she has lost.

My father's favorite song is "Amazing Grace." Whenever I hear it, I cry, not only because the song itself is moving but also because

I know the day will come when I hear that song played at my father's funeral, that I will be left to sing it when he exists no longer in this world. He knows the words to "Amazing Grace," not all the verses, but for sure the chorus, and he sings it with feeling, not caring whether he can hit the high notes or even the low notes but seemingly just grateful for the song, a song promising that what is lost will be found, a song promising to bring us home.

Some ten years after my mother lost the hearing in her right ear, my father lost the hearing in his left. One day while practicing yoga, taking a difficult arm balance, half of his hearing just disappeared. Like magic. The doctors have no idea how or why, but they are not all that alarmed. At the age of seventy-five, apparently it's not that uncommon to wake up one day to a much quieter world. My parents have been married for over fifty years; the time they did not know one another occupies a sliver of their existence. When they stand side-by-side, as they did in front of the priest almost sixty years ago, they can hear sound coming from both the right and the left.

I have learned to place myself between them.

Recently I met a woman who works with those who face terrible diseases like ALS—diseases that take one's ability to walk, to move, to hug your children. When asked, those who suffer often say that the loss of hearing causes them the most pain. Cut off from the world around them, having never learned alternate ways to communicate or unable to master this new skill late in life, they become alienated and depressed. My father, once the most dominating presence in a room, has visibly thinned in the past three years. Forever cupping his hand around his left ear, body straining forward, the look I see often on his face resembles confusion, an expression he rarely wore in my childhood. Half a beat behind the joke, behind the pun, behind the dramatic turn in a story, my father has receded. I cannot tell you the last time I heard him sing.

Because he cannot hear as well as he once could, I have turned to words. I write him a letter every week, stories from the days with my family, my Michael and the boys. I try to write about subjects that I think he will find meaningful—Aidan's math competitions or Kellen's most recent project at school. I don't write about painful things, don't tell him my darkest worries, but I do work to invite him into our lives, provide fragments that work like bridges, bridges made of words that do not have to be heard to be held.

I teach yoga twice a week at a local studio, and I begin every class by chanting. I learned to chant in India, where all yoga classes start this way, with song. In yoga, you chant mantras, Sanskrit words that are sacred and most often invoke the Divine in all of us. Mantras are energy based, not word based. In fact, language only points toward the sound; letters cannot embody the sound. They approximate. Not unlike the breath, mantra gives your mind a place to focus, a way to still its busy chatter. The students who chant with me probably don't realize how sacred the words are, but they love that part of class and have memorized the lines. Those who are new to my class often come up to me afterward and tell me that I have a beautiful voice. I cannot hear what they hear, but I am grateful.

Each time I chant, I feel as though I am uttering an incantation. The words create a space, which then is held, not unlike the spell cast by narrative, the voice of the essayist who carries the reader from the first word to the last. In yoga the words I sing are thousands of years old. They have been chanted by millions and millions of people, across continents and class and countries and time. Every time I chant them, I am chanting with an unnamed number of others around the world who are practicing with me. The world vibrates.

The song I sing at the end of class, the *twameva*, is a Sanskrit lullaby of sorts. Traditionally it was sung by monks who had renounced everything in the world in order to devote their lives to God. A simple but beautiful chant, it begins, "You are my mother. You are my father." For the devotee, the words mean they have left their own mother and father and taken God as their only parent. When I chant this song, float the syllables across the bodies of my students in *savasana*, I think of my mother and father and how much of my life I owe to them. For the words they gave me and the words they forgot. For the words heard and the ones read. For words set to music and words spoken only in the heart. I wish more than anything that their hearing could be fully restored, but, much like the past itself, what hearing they have will remain partial and all that I have.

My sons can sing the fragments to scores of songs, some of them the same fragments my father handed down to me, some that I have marooned on my own. When I would sing them to sleep at night, there were only two or three songs that I could sing in their entirety. Most often we eddied in the refrain. I could always sense the moment when my sons fell asleep. Their breathing changed, deepened. I would continue singing over their sleeping bodies, casting a spell of word and sound that I believed they could still hear, even as they drifted into dream. Those bits of song, those incantations, are, I hope, still singing in their blood. Even if the words are gone, even if the hearing is halved, surely the spell remains.

Sky Song

The voice you heard was right, says
Vedanta, but the direction you gave
to the voice was wrong; that ideal of
freedom that you perceived was correct
but you projected it outside yourself and
that was your mistake. Bring it nearer
and nearer until you find that it was all
the time within you.

—Swami Vivekananda

The turtle looked dead, head down, wedged in the crack at the bottom of the shark exhibit; its rear end bobbed in the manufactured currents.

"Do you think he's okay?" I asked Kellen. "Maybe he's sleeping."

At eleven, Kellen no longer inhabited a world where dead things were asleep and Santa came through the front door when a chimney was unavailable. He shook his head. "We need to tell someone."

I looked around the shark tunnel for an employee but met only our reflections in the glass. Nurse sharks and leopards swam through our hearts, a shovelnose skimmed our hairlines. The tunnel, empty, save for us. We had been first in line that morning when the aquarium opened, having driven under a cloudless sky the two hours from Logan, Utah, to Draper. Kellen didn't want to miss a minute, made us skip Starbucks, and kept asking to see my phone to check the time as we stood before locked doors. Once our tickets were purchased, we headed straight for the shark tunnel, while Kellen chattered about hammerheads, lemons, and bull sharks. Instead we found a giant sea turtle, bobbing upside down, golden belly exposed, pale white skin showing where flippers met the shell, dead.

"Bubble butt," the man told us when we finally tracked down a blue-uniformed aquarium worker near the touch pool. "He was bit by a shark in the wild, and when his shell grew back it trapped a bubble of air inside so now he has trouble keeping himself submerged."

"But his head," I said, remembering how it was wedged into the crack at the base of the wall. Such an odd angle, so violent.

"They do that so that they can sleep at night."

"See, he *was* sleeping!" I said to Kellen, trying to glide past the fact that the shark-attacked turtle now inhabited a shark tank. "Only sleeping."

Kellen said nothing.

We returned to the shark tank, little reassured by the diagnosis. The turtle was gone. We both looked up but could not see to the surface because of the glare from the lights. "Where did he go?" I wondered aloud. Other visitors pointed to the colorful fish and the rays gliding, belly flat, to the glass. I wanted to tell them about the turtle, point to the rock where he had wedged his head. "He was right there."

Over a nine-year period, he produced four hundred surviving prints in the series, beginning in 1922 and ending in 1931—prolific years for him—a rebirth of sorts. The photographs are all small—measuring four by five inches—so you must move close to see them—you must bring your body, with its hair, smells, and limits, into proximity with the equally cropped sky. Alfred Stieglitz wanted it that way, wanted the viewer—wanted the *viewing*—to be a physical experience—more than physical, religious, so that the one who looked, looked with her entire being, could be enlightened, saved. The artist himself had to gaze up to capture the clouds and then down to develop the negative. He knew the relationship between the macro and micro—heft of camera, push of wind, slant of sun; he had watched that particular line of sky for a lifetime. Smaller than a wedding invitation, his sky songs were meant to pull the viewer into a vortex of light, merging the immediate and the transcendent.

After 1925 he called them Equivalents. But he also called them "music;" he called them "beautiful," "snapshots," and both "a vision of life" and his "philosophy of life." He called them "great sky stories" and "documents of eternal relationships." In a famous letter to Hart Crane, he said he had photographed God.

His clouds do not record the weather. They do not document the day or the season or the sky. They are not clouds at all. Or at least not only. They are representational and abstract. Disorienting. Sometimes, it is unclear that you are even looking at the sky. The images could be hung in any direction—down and up no longer useful terms, no compass, no orientation, no narrative to hold onto. Of his photographs—of his clouds in particular—Stieglitz says, "What is of greatest importance is to hold a moment, to record something so completely that those who see it will relive an equivalent of what has been expressed."

Eknath Easwaran, a translator and spiritual teacher, calls the Upanishads "snapshots of towering peaks of consciousness." Written in verse, they are hymns of/to the unknown, the unknowable, handed down for thousands of years. He goes on to suggest that those who have seen similar peaks will recognize the view. They will nod their heads with every line. That is it.

The Upanishads affirm that Reality can be experienced directly, through meditation, without the need for rituals or priests. One must rely on one-pointed focus (*dhyana*) and work passionately in a single direction (*tapas*). Ironically, Reality (our oneness with everything) exists as "our native state," but we remain ignorant of that joy. Instead, we fill our days with the finite, content with the frames we are given, limited by what can be seen through the lens. We sit atop the treasure and then look around for gold. The Upanishads tell us, "There is no joy in the finite; there is only joy in the infinite." The ice cream cone appeases for a moment, before regret or desire returns. The new dress is barely out of the bag before dissatisfaction and restlessness take up roost. We fail to see what stands before us—the fact that the Divine infuses everything and we are one with that limitlessness.

Kellen and I spent the rest of the morning looking for slender fire gobies, waiting for the zebra mantis shrimp to smash its prey, and comparing the crusher claws on the American lobster; we sat as the penguins rolled rocks around their exhibit and later stood while the otters were fed fish scraps. But the whole time I remained with the turtle, the one I had thought was dead but wasn't, the one who wedged head into rock every night, the one born to the earth, mothered by the sea, and who now contained the sky.

Later I would learn the dangers of bubble butt syndrome. Turtles in the wild—attacked by sharks or the props of boats—often die because they can no longer submerge themselves to feed or to escape. A turtle's shell is not really shell but spine, so the air can't be "released" by piercing without causing paralysis. The pocket of air, sky, remains a part of the turtle for life. If a turtle with bubble butt is rescued then weights can be attached to its shell—in the same tank another turtle swam with a small backpack of weights across his back as if he were setting off for school. The turtle can then sink to the floor. Or it can learn to adapt to its new buoyancy by anchoring into the reef at night. But its energy, after the trauma, is forever upward, the air in its shell longing to be reunited with the sky.

Stieglitz spent his life preparing for the Equivalents. They are the sum total of what he learned in forty years of holding a camera. Stieglitz dedicated decades—a lifetime—to establishing photography as an art form—not in relation to painting, not in relation to music—but a medium with its own vocabulary and language. Photography, he argued, was more than mechanics, more than documentation. Photographs could be, he wrote to Sherwood Anderson, "a reality—so subtle that it becomes more real than reality." Images could capture the center of the center of the target.

The story goes that the Equivalents were a response to a statement by Waldo Frank suggesting that Stieglitz hypnotized those who sat for him—photography as trickery more than art. In an essay about the cloud series, Stieglitz gives eight reasons for turning his attention to the sky. Not one of them convinces. Stieglitz had already confronted every technical challenge presented by photography—taking pictures in the night, in the rain, in the snow. He had, he writes, after all, been watching clouds his entire life. The Equivalents don't derive from any external force or pressure—no reason exists for their genesis. Instead they arise, as all art must, Stieglitz affirms, from "inner need." "It is," he says, "not until a need presents itself—until individuals feel it within—that anything meaningful can happen."

In the early 1920s, he faced disintegration: his beloved mother dying, the family estate falling apart, a country recovering from war. But he also found rebirth—the love affair with Georgia O'Keeffe—a white hot heat. ("Have you ever been in love? Then you can photograph.") Amid desolation and passion, on the shores of a lake where his lover swam and his mother's health failed, he turned his camera to the sky.

"His face is everywhere," the Upanishads assure.

Your face is everywhere. Looking into another's eyes, you meet your own.

A second irony of the Upanishads, first an orally transmitted and then a written text, arises from the knowledge that the realization of the unknown, the unmanifest, occurs outside the bounds of language. You cannot read and know. The experience of Reality—"That from which all words turn back and thoughts can never reach"—escapes translation. A more recent teacher of Vedanta, Sri Ramakrishna, writes, "He reasons about It as long as he has not realized it." The talking, the writing, the asserting all come before. Scriptures become straw, Ramakrishna says, once Reality is known. That knowing can only come through the heart, rather than the mind. It is felt rather than articulated. And once you have realized it, you want to share what you have experienced. So you search for a way.

By the time we reached Sardine Canyon, I was tired of driving. The interstate runs between Logan and Draper, an easy drive, but the day at the aquarium had been long, and I was looking forward to just being home. For most of the drive, Kellen passed the time playing video games on his iPod. I made him put the device away once we left the straight roads. Sardine Canyon passes through the Wasatch Front to the valley where Logan sits. A four-lane divided highway that climbs to seven thousand feet, the pass takes lives every year. People die, mostly on icy roads, but also from inattention and speed and the lack of a consistent barrier dividing the lanes traveling north and south. Because Kellen suffers from motion sickness, I wanted his eyes on the road.

He sat next to me in the front. In his lap, he held the remote-controlled shark he had convinced me to buy when the aquarium routed our exit through the gift shop.

"Should we try him in the bathtub when we get home?" I asked.

"Or a big plastic bin," he said.

I imagined all that would need to be dumped.

"Let's turn on the radio," I suggested, just as we left the final stoplight in Brigham City and headed into the canyon proper. I drove in the right lane. We climbed, gaining speed.

Kellen pushed the buttons on the radio, fiddling with the balance and the bass.

I looked down to see what station he had landed on. In that moment, the car ahead of me changed lanes. When I looked back up, I saw the rear end of a slow-moving van coming at us, only we were the ones hurtling through space and the van was the one standing still.

I slammed on the brakes and felt the car shudder. We weren't going to stop in time.

Stieglitz once quipped of academics and critics, "The trouble with these people is that they know so damned much they experience nothing—so know really nothing." For Stieglitz, physical experience was at the very root of what it meant to be human. Though he did not often cite the Transcendentalists before him, his understanding of the natural world as evidence of the Eternal and our connections to one another aligns with their thinking. He favored art grounded in physical reality and often saw much of the work being done by abstractionists as "dead." This didn't mean his work was always representational—for example, the Equivalents are not—but rather that art must be a living thing, something that could be re-experienced again and again. A photograph was not meant simply to document reality but to convey what the artist experienced in the seeing—and then mediate a similar experience for the viewer. In that way, art was alive. It was not an end, a product, but a beginning, a conversation, one that could be passed down. ("I am not interested in anything which is not thoroughly alive."). To Hart Crane he wrote, "I also know that there is more of the really abstract in some 'representation' than in most of the dead representations in the so called abstract so fashionable now."

The importance of the physicality of experience can be seen in how he arranged his galleries, what he asked each viewer to undertake—a journey out of language and into the ecstatic—where emptiness was often the only appropriate response. His galleries had posted hours of silence, like a monastery. His Equivalents, like nuns, matted in white coifs. The walls were often bare. Kristina Wilson writes, "He wanted not an art that simply illustrated the complete spiritual state but one that catalyzed the process of enlightenment." For Stieglitz, "all true art is a religious manifestation"—in the way that it connects the viewer to the inexpressible—the artist first experiences the unfathomable and then creates an image that allows the viewer to see (really see) Truth. The initial experience between artist and subject and the secondary experience between art and viewer occur without mediator, without translation, without word. Late in his life, Stieglitz said, "You will discover that if the artist could explain in words what he has made, he would not have created." Because only the direct and unmediated experience matters, he draws the viewer close to his Equivalents. Not even air can be between. Not unlike enlightenment itself: direct, experiential, and outside of language.

In a letter to Paul Rosenfield in 1923, at the onset of his Equivalents, he wrote, "I'm not sure about being as much an artist as one of the leading spiritual forces of this country." While the claim is steeped in arrogance, it clearly demonstrates his desire to move beyond even the abstraction and capture what cannot be caught.

Swami Tyagananda, a monk of the Ramakrishna Order and the head of the Vedanta Society in the United States, lectures weekly from Boston and travels around the world. In a lecture entitled "Why Believe in God," he makes the point that we cannot deny what we do not know. If you say you don't believe in God, he will ask you to describe your concept of God. Most likely he will answer that he doesn't believe in that God either. We can, he says, only discredit what we know. And the Divine is hard to realize. It's all right there, right before us, but instead we create separation, largely through language, cordoning reality into the things we can see, feel, and hear. If you do realize God, through meditation or maybe through a single flash, you won't be able to tell anyone about it. The unmanifest, by definition, exists beyond concept. Each person must realize the Divine on their own. There can be no agreement over attributes, no shared concept, because the realization is particular and personal. But once you have experienced oneness, Swami Tyagananda says, you will know—not in your mind, but in your heart. He says, "It is not what you believe that matters, it is what you know." He goes on to say, "What matters is what you have experienced of God in the depths your heart."

Here is what will happen in under a second: You will think, I cannot stop in time. You will think, I must move to the right because traffic pulses to my left. You will move to the right. You will think, I have to hold the car on the shoulder. You will be unable to hold the car on the shoulder. You will think, I cannot move too far to the right: ravine, and trees, and an end. You will move to the left, and the car will swing violently. Your body will rock back and forth. You will say to your child, sitting next to you, holding his remote-controlled shark, no, no longer holding, the shark now flying through the car, you will say, "It's going to be okay." You will say this because you will remember your husband, Michael, saying this when you flipped your canoe three years ago in the freezing water of the Little Bear river. You will remember how he said this when the boys' heads, your sons, popped up amid the rapids, eyes white with alarm and cold. You will remember that while you thought "swim," Michael thought to reassure, so you will say, "It's going to be okay," out loud, shark swimming past, as the car swerves back and forth on the road, rubber screaming against pavement. You will hear the car hit the guardrail. You will feel the solidity of that rail, the thunk and crunch. You will see the trees coming at you, barely dressed in green, so early in the spring, trunks and limbs skeletal but thick. And below them, the ravine. You will hold tight to the steering wheel, will it to keep you out of the oncoming traffic, out of the trees, out of the ravine. You will beg the car, low and heavy, shelled, to keep you tethered to the earth.

Stieglitz described one of his Equivalents as "reaching up beyond the sun, the living point, into darkness, which is also light." To say he embraced contradiction misses the point. Light and shadow weren't contradictory for Stieglitz; they were the same, one. Time and again, he insisted to other photographers that one only needed the barest amount of light to photograph. By stopping down his camera, decreasing the size of the aperture and therefore the amount of light coming in, Stieglitz found light where others saw only shadow. Light was always there for Stieglitz, even in the dark, even when human eyes could not detect it and the mind refused to see it. Toward the end of his life, Stieglitz said, "There is with me ever an affirmation of light. Thus, no matter how much black there may be in the world, I experience tragedy, beauty, but never futility. I am aware of the duality, the ambiguity of world forces at work. Yet it is when conflict hovers about a point, a focal point, and light is in the ascendancy, that I feel the necessity to photograph." Mother dying, estate failing, and a lover whose body he knew through both lens and hand, Stieglitz cropped the sky to create images that moved outward *because* they had been limited, moved into desolation and ecstasy in order to "make visible the invisible." They are not God but the realization of God—what it felt like for him to realize the unity of light and dark, earth and sky, I and you.

Nothing happened when I took Jesus into my heart at the age of ten. The Sunday School teacher who stood before us seemed so certain of the joy that would come when I did. "Invite him into your heart," she told the class, and I imagined my heart door swinging open on a hinge, Jesus becoming small so that he could fit through such a tiny passage. And he would remain there, she assured us. We only had to ask him once.

So I closed my eyes that Sunday, and I stood up from the bench to elongate the opening in my chest. "Please come into my heart," I said to Jesus. With eyes squeezed shut I begged in a way I had never begged for anything—not a Holly Hobbie Oven or a Baby Alive or the new Sunshine Family. I wanted that promised joy so much, but it never came. I knew my heart was too little for the brown-haired Jesus framed in the entryway to the Subase Chapel, the one lifting a Navy submarine from the depths of the ocean, rays of sunlight bouncing from the hull and shooting into the golden sun. He inhabited the sky, and no matter how tall I stood I remained earthbound.

When the car came to a rest, we found ourselves trapped between three enormous steel cables. The guard rail, it turned out, was not an actual rail, but rather three thick wires running parallel to the ground. Somehow the car had lifted over two of the cables, knocked down several posts, and now sat between those two cables and the third one. A single wire kept us from the void. The windshield wipers flashed across the glass.

"Are you okay?" I asked Kellen.

He nodded.

I could see no blood, no scrapes. He no longer held anything in his hands, but other than that he looked the same to me. Drivers began to stop, yelled to us, "Are you okay?"

I kept nodding, saying we were fine. I imagined that somehow we would just start the car and return to the road. Catch our breaths, shake our heads, and move on. When I tried to open the doors, though, I found I could not because the tension on the wires had trapped us inside. Then I began to cry.

Overheard by Dorothy Norman at Stieglitz's gallery, An American Place:

> MAN (looking at a Stieglitz Equivalent): "Is this a photograph of water?"
>
> AS: "What difference does it make of what it is a photograph?"
>
> MAN: "But is it a photograph of water?"
>
> AS: "I tell you it does not matter."
>
> MAN: "Well then is it a picture of the sky?"
>
> AS: "It happens to be a picture of the sky. But I cannot understand why that is of any consequence."

Swami Tyagananda says whichever idea of God makes sense to you, hold onto it. If that is Reason, so be it. If that is a mountain, fine. An elephant, a goddess, the clouds that hover just above the hills surrounding Lake George in late August, hold tight. For only by holding fast to your idea of God can you ever hope to access the Reality that your idea represents. It won't be the same idea that others carry—and for that be grateful. The Reality itself will be the same, the same oneness that we all have the opportunity to realize. Take whatever vehicle carries you to that oneness. One of the four *mahavakyas*—great teachings—of the Upanishads is *tat tvam asi*.

You are That.

Tat, "that," arrives intentionally vague, empty but therefore full: barely a word, a whisper really, the fewest strokes possible, the least space taken, a small slant of light, a nimbus, an aperture stopped down, a turtle, a cloud, the pale cheeks of your son who reassures you that everything will be okay, your son, the skid marks on the road, the road itself, and the demolished guardrail, the molten sky at dawn when you run, the star-dark sky canopied over the sleeping shark, the shark, and the tangle of silver fish in the tank, the line of sky you have studied half your lifetime, the careening car, the flying car, the car that holds the ground, the little girl standing in the Quonset hut, the woman who looks away for a moment, and the one who never turns her head. You are That.

The moment before the accident, the moment when we were still headed up the canyon toward home, the moment when we still stood on the side of the line we knew as this world, I looked down to see what station Kellen had chosen on the radio. The radio, while not fancy, did give the first three words to the title of the song being played. The word I saw before I looked back up to the van, all caps, was "GOD."

Stieglitz writes of his Equivalents, "I can do nothing because another does it, nothing that is not for me to do because of some deep inner need. I clarify for myself alone. I am interested in putting down an image only of what I have seen, not what it means to me. It is only after I have put down an equivalent of what has moved me, that I can even begin to think about its meaning . . . I feel that all experiences in life in any particular form must be an equivalent of any other truly felt experience."

When asked what a perfect photograph was, Stieglitz responded: "I will be sitting with the plate of a picture I have just taken in my hands. It will be the picture I have always known that some day I would be able to take. It will be the perfect photograph, embodying all that I have ever wished to say. I will have just developed it, just have looked at it, just have seen that it was exactly what I wanted. The room will be empty, quiet. The walls will be bare—clean. I will sit looking at the picture. It will slip from my hands, and break as it falls to the ground. I will be dead. They will come. No one will ever have seen the picture nor known what it was."

Durga, the Hindu goddess mother, rides like a warrior into battle on a lion. She stomped out demons that no male god could conquer and birthed Kali, goddess of destruction. She is the goddess you call on for protection and my Ishta Devata, my chosen image for the Divine. In my early morning meditations, I often meditate on Durga, envision her encasing my body in gold light, shielding me from harm. Armor clad, demon slayer, mother, she does not placate or soothe. Her love is teethed.

As the car slid from the road, in that second in which my mind calculated direction and distance and relative speed, the traffic, the shoulder width, and the rate of deceleration, the second in which I somehow knew that the car, heavy like a tank, was not going to roll over, that it would hold to the ground, I thought I told my son that it was going to be okay. I thought I said those words out loud. And maybe I did. Kellen doesn't remember me saying that, but he also doesn't remember much. He remembers sage brush coming at him and the windshield wipers sweeping dirty glass. For days, I carried this version of the story—the one in which I reassured my child as the world broke apart. The other day, while meditating, though, I found myself back in that swerving vehicle. I felt the car weave madly from side to side, shark swimming past, trees reaching bare limbs

toward our bodies like claws, and I heard those words again—
"It's going to be okay." Only they did not come from my lips, but
rather were whispered in my ear. Whispered from inside of me
and also to me, a reassurance more certain than the steel cables
that kept us from the edge.

CODA

Hurt People Hurt People

When I pick Aidan up from school, he hurls his backpack into the car like it's a body. Slamming the back door shut, he joins me in the front, brown hair curtaining eyes I know better than my own.

"How was school?" I ask.

"Terrible."

School is not normally terrible for my fourteen-year-old son, especially now that he has begun high school. In years prior, when he attended a small charter school that favored worksheets and math facts and sitting on your pockets, Aidan would climb into the car already in tears. Since starting at Logan High, student population 1,100, he has only loved it.

Until today.

"What happened?" I ask.

Aidan remains quiet while we exit the school parking lot and turn onto streets lined with fall-colored trees. Above, the sky stretches lapis blue, rinsed and empty of clouds. In northern Utah, early October has no equal.

I don't push, know that we sit at the conversational fork. If he goes left, I will learn no more. Right, and he might open.

Waiting is hard for me.

"Promise you won't get upset?" he asks.

Two days later, my close friend Jen, whose son is older than Aidan, will tell me never to make that promise.

"I promise."

Aidan says nothing. We drive slowly through the neighborhood. An earlier rain has pasted maple leaves into a yellow path that we follow past brick homes.

"Do you promise?" he asks again.

"Did you fail your math test?"

Nothing.

"Did you drink a bunch of soda?"

These examples will remain with me in the following weeks, the parameters of the world I inhabited on a Monday afternoon in early October, the world in which soda played the villain.

"No, Mom. I was hit."

I step on the brakes and look over at him, mouth open.

"You promised."

When I pull the car over, we are only two blocks from the school. Forget promises.

I learn that in debate class earlier that day a student named Carson had been denigrating debate and those who spent weekends at debate tournaments. Even though he was on the team, he had chosen to stay home partying and watching football. In the past Carson had been verbally aggressive toward Aidan, mocking him for the work he was doing on his speeches, deriding him for his efforts. Aidan, on the other hand, was fast finding a home in that group, loved tracking down details about civil asset forfeiture and China as a trade partner. That afternoon, Carson must have reached his limit; he turned on Aidan directly and called him stupid.

The five students who make up student congress were by themselves in a room—they call it the Think Tank—off the main classroom. No teachers were present.

Aidan told Carson that football was crap.

Carson walked over to where Aidan was sitting, cornered him in the small room, drew back, and slapped Aidan across the face.

The Conquest of Sumer, the Conquest of Sargon, the Persian
War, the Peloponnesian War

"Let me see," I say to Aidan as we sit parked.

His cheek glows red, but I cannot tell if that redness comes
from the smack or the confusion that clearly circulates through
his body.

"We have to tell someone," I say.

"No, no way," Aidan responds, and his eyes accuse me for doing
the very thing he knew I would do.

"We have to, Aidan. I don't know what will happen, but I
know deep in my heart that you must say something."

A few days earlier Christine Blasey Ford testified against Brett
Kavanaugh. Her voice remains with me in the car as I sit with
Aidan, the voice that shook as she answered in the simplest of
words how certain she was that Kavanaugh had assaulted her:
"One hundred percent." One hundred percent certain that Kavanaugh was the one who held his hand over her mouth so that
she wouldn't scream while he tried to rape her. Maybe it is his
hand, more than her voice, that makes me urge Aidan forward.
The hand that prevented her words then.

Aidan insists we enter the school through the west doors rather
than the main entrance. "I don't want to see anyone I know," he
says. The halls are empty; school has been out for twenty minutes.
But I walk all the way around the school to the west doors with
my son because he has agreed to speak.

The counselor's first words are, "Well, that is clearly way, way,
way over the line."

"It's assault," I say.

He doesn't disagree.

The counselor works with 350 students—students with last names S to Z. Around his desk, his family gathers in framed photos; really, they gather around him. He forms the center, his children flanking him and his wife. I have lived in Utah for twenty years and know how to read the surfaces: he is a member of the Church of Jesus Christ of Latter-day Saints. This means little except that it puts him, most probably, in line with the politics of this state, the state with two senators who vehemently supported Kavanaugh from day one, the state that requires a seventy-two-hour waiting period for women who choose an abortion and then requires that they return to Salt Lake City for the procedure, the state that allows students in my university classrooms to carry weapons with concealed carry permits.

The counselor is kind; he expresses concern even if his language of "crossing the line" and my language of "assault" fail to meet. He tells Aidan that he will remove Carson from his classes, meet with Carson and the witnesses in the morning, have the resource officer take his statement.

"Does that sound okay?" I ask Aidan. I have made him tell the story, made him describe the way it felt to be slapped.

"I'm just worried about what will happen once Carson knows I've said something."

The counselor tells Aidan that he will try to ensure that Carson doesn't know who stepped forward.

"My son's fourteen," I say. "In his whole life he has never been hit by anyone, not even his younger brother."

"Just stay in open places."

Anita Sarkeesian, a feminist and outspoken media critic, chose not to speak at my university in October of 2014 when she learned that weapons were allowed on campus. Emails had been sent to several university faculty and staff promising violence against Sarkeesian and all the feminists in the audience if Sarkeesian was allowed to talk. In fact, one of the emails threatened "the deadliest school shooting in American history." The university said it could do nothing to prevent people with concealed carry permits from attending the event. The only protection they could offer Sarkeesian was to forbid large backpacks.

When Jen and I learned Sarkeesian had canceled her appearance, we wrote a letter to the university president articulating the slim distance between silencing speakers and silencing faculty in the classroom. More than one hundred faculty signed the letter, enraged over both censorship and the presence of guns. But nothing could be done. Utah was the very first state in the country to allow concealed weapons on college campuses, and it remains the only state that specifically names colleges and universities as "nonexempt" from the law.

In the days following our letter, Jen and I fielded calls from reporters all over the country. Television crews asked to come to our house. Online comments grew hostile and aggressive. We began to fear that those who sent the emails threatening violence to anyone who spoke against them would find our houses, draw near to our sons. Within three days of sending the letter to the president, we both agreed to remain silent about the issue for our own safety and the safety of our families. We returned no more calls, gave no more interviews, stayed inside.

War of Alexander the Great, Punic War, Gallic War, Caesar's invasion of Britain, Great Jewish Revolt, Yellow Turban Rebellion, War against the Moors in North Africa, Roman-Persian War

Michael and I huddle together the night after Carson hits Aidan and talk about guns, how many there are in this state—close to a million permits in a state with only three million inhabitants. More to the point, Utah was recently ranked the lowest of all fifty states in gun-control legislation. The only state in the union that has language in its constitution that forbids any law that might interfere with gun ownership, its law reads "no entity may enact, establish, or enforce any ordinance, regulation, rule, or policy pertaining to firearms that in any way inhibits or restricts the possession or use of firearms on either public or private property."

I have lived in Utah for so long at this point that I no longer have a frame of reference for what it might mean to reside in a blue state or even a purple one. Perhaps there are other parents, maybe those more informed or less informed, who would not move from their son being slapped at school to images of him being sought out and then shot in the cafeteria. I am not that mother. I live in this state.

"Michael," I ask, "do we send him back to school tomorrow?"

"I don't know," Michael answers.

We are sitting at the kitchen table, and my laptop is open in front of me. Together we have composed an email to the school asking them to take action. We write, "When we put our son on the bus in the morning, we are turning his safety and well-being over to you."

"Do we say anything about guns specifically?" I ask Michael.

The day before, in the counselor's office, I alluded to the possibility of "further consequences" because I didn't want to use the word gun in front of Aidan.

In the end, we write about our fear of guns and the fact that, after school shootings, everyone always says there were signs.

"This IS a sign," we write. Then hit send.

Aidan tells us before he heads out the door for the bus the following morning that Carson talks incessantly about war and guns. It is everything I can do not to grab him by the arm and pull him back inside the house. Bigger than me, he could easily escape my grasp, but I think he would stay home if I insisted.

Michael and I both kiss him good-bye and watch him head down the dark street.

Byzantine-Arab War, Muslim Conquest of Egypt, First Siege of
Constantinople, Arab-Chinese War, Saxon Wars, Viking raids
across Europe, Bulgarian Siege of Constantinople, Zanj Rebellion in southern Iraq, Croatian-Bulgarian War, Viking Civil War,
Norman Conquest of England

In the twenty minutes between seeing Aidan off at the door and
taking Kellen to seventh grade, I read the daily entry in Mark
Nepo's *The Book of Awakening*. A spiritual seeker, poet, and cancer survivor, Nepo speaks with authority about the need to stay
present and love because everything leaves.

The reading for this Tuesday begins with a Zen story. A man has
a beautiful bird, both sweet and dear. He wants to protect the bird
so he places it in a glass container. For a long time, the bird happily
sings to him all day long. But then the bird grows and grows, soon
filling its cage. The man comes to understand that the only way to
free the bird is to break the jar, killing his song spinner.

The bird, Nepo writes, represents the heart; the glass container,
the mind. Too often we try to protect and control the things we
love, the world around us, but the heart cannot be contained. It
will wither and die if the mind refuses to let it go. The heart lives
boundless, never meant to be caged. My sparrow-dark son now
sits on the bus, the one that will take him back to the high school
with the open floor plan, enormous glass windows, and wide halls.

"For the next few days," the counselor told Aidan the day
before, "I would encourage you to stay in groups, never be alone."

First Crusade, Second Crusade, Third Crusade, Fourth Crusade,
Children's Crusade, Fifth, Sixth, Seventh, Eighth, Ninth Crusade

We say nothing to Kellen. The day it happens I tell him that
Aidan had a hard day at school and he should maybe ask him
about it.

"I don't know," Kellen says, "How could I help him?"

Someday, perhaps the two of them will confide in each another, find the bond that they had when they were younger and could play LEGOS or Bakugan for hours and hours. They don't interact much at this age. The two years between them, simultaneously too close and too far. Kellen hovers at the edge of the family, while Aidan plays out the drama of his days at the dinner table. It does not surprise me that Kellen can't imagine being of help to Aidan. Aidan has long watched out for him.

Kellen and I are driving to school, my heart with Aidan.

"When is the election again?" Kellen asks out of the blue.

"November 6," I say.

"And what do we need to impeach Trump?" he asks.

I am in the midst of explaining what would have to happen in the House when my phone rings. The screen on the dashboard reads "Logan High."

I hit the button to transfer the call to the phone and answer.

"Officer Beven here," comes the deep voice, "I'm calling about an incident that involved your son and another student."

Driving through the sleepy roads of Logan, I consider pulling over to take the call but know that Kellen would hate being late, so I continue.

The officer tells me that he is going to call Carson in to see him. "If the witnesses support your son's story," he says, "this is assault."

"Yes, it is," I confirm, glad that the officer and I agree on vocabulary. No line crossing here.

"Would you like to press charges?"

And here is when I unravel, driving the Subaru under another fall-bright sky. I'm not sure why. Maybe the legal language or the opportunity for action or this man giving us a choice that seems less like a choice and more like a sentence. This is the moment I no longer feel like I am in control.

"What would it even mean to press charges?" I begin, and then, before he can answer, continue as I roll through the only stop sign left between home and Kellen's school, "And why would another student do this? He needs help. This is illegal. We, as a society, have said that you cannot communicate this way. By hitting. It's illegal. Aidan didn't do anything. At all. And he has never been hit. I am forty-nine, I have never been hit. My son has been. That breaks my heart. My son has been. I am forty-nine. And we live in this state. This state with guns. How can you protect my son? From guns? From someone with a gun who seeks him out? He's fourteen. And there are guns. And he has been hit."

Then I look over at Kellen. His cheeks are pale, eyes down.

"The only tool I have," the officer continues, "is if you press charges."

The only weapon I have, is what I hear.

We arrive at Kellen's school, and I mouth good-bye to him. He is opening the door before the car even halts, fleeing.

"I don't want Carson to know that Aidan was the one who said something."

"If you press charges," Office Beven says, "then there's a chance that Aidan will have to testify in court against the accuser. Are you okay with that? He would be named."

Blasey Ford studies trauma, the acute psychological kind, the breaking that happens after war or rape or physical assault, the kind that lodges in the amygdala, the primitive part of our brains, where experiences are stored in image rather than language, the breaking so complete that there are no words. As a scholar, she understands the totality of the wounding. As a survivor, she knows the feel. "Indelible in the hippocampus is the laughter," she testified in front of the Senate, "the uproarious laughter between the two." Ford was assaulted by Kavanaugh. Of this, I have little doubt. In the few times in my life I have been sexually violated—

either direct abuse from my grandfather or the typical abuse all women experience, groping, fondling, leering, pressing—I remember everything. Even at the age of seven, on the tractor, my grandfather's hand rubbing my nipples. You do not forget.

People asked why Blasey Ford didn't do anything at the time of the event, why her parents didn't do anything. These people want her to be a different person, bear her wound differently. Her story is denied now because she didn't step forward then.

"We'll press charges."

> Norman invasion of Ireland, Mongol invasion of China, Mongol invasion of Afghanistan, Mongol invasion of Vietnam, the Hundred Years War, Chinese Domination of Vietnam, Polish-Lithuanian-Teutonic War, Hunger War, Fall of Constantinople, Wars of the Roses, War of the Priests, Muscovite-Lithuanian War, The Spanish Conquest of Mexico, The Mughal Conquest of India, War of the Two Brothers

Michael sounds upset when I call him minutes after hanging up with Officer Beven. "You can't make decisions like that on your own!"

I am parked, about to go to yoga.

"I'm sorry," I say, "I didn't think it through. He said it was the only option."

"It's not the only option," Michael says. "We have to deescalate the situation. Not escalate. We don't want to push that kid into thinking a gun is the only answer."

"I'm sorry. I'm sorry." Parked and alone in the car, it seems obvious that I should have told the officer I would call him back.

"It's fine," Michael reassures. "You were just making an executive decision. But if we press charges that will remain on that kid's record for life. These things are felonies now, not misdemeanors."

"But what if something happens to Aidan? We will never forgive ourselves for not being more aggressive." And then I cry.

"There are no second chances with guns," I said to Beven as I unraveled earlier that morning. And I kept seeing Aidan, my dear sweet boy, the one who cried every time we left him at day care, the one who still sleeps with a stufftie, who brings pictures of his cat with him when we travel, the one who asks us to remember to write him notes on his dry-erase board every morning, who worries that no one will trick-or-treat with him at his age, who cried so hard when he found out that Santa was not real that I turned around from the airport where I was about to board a plane and drove the two hours home, the boy with hazel eyes deep like the juniper-covered mountains that surround the house he has lived in his entire life. I kept seeing that boy, my boy, crumple to the ground, blood coming from his chest, draining through his fingers.

Michael taught me to believe in a second chance for everyone. I had been a liberal when we met in graduate school but hadn't yet understood that everyone was sacred, even those who harmed. I didn't believe in the Divine at all, was a safe, intellectual atheist. I worked with my mind. I contained. Ironically, it would take moving to Zion before I began to believe that I was being watched over.

I wish I could remember the details of the conversation, the film we were talking about. I have looked back over the films released in 1997 and 1998—*The Ice Storm, The Thin Red Line*—but I can't remember what prompted the discussion. I know we were walking in the bare-naked woods in late winter, not far from the Huron River. Snow still patched the ground and the sky was cinerous, low. It was right at freezing, and I wore every layer I could garner from my graduate school winter wardrobe. Michael walked beside me, his long body close to mine, our relationship not yet a year old.

I was arguing for life in prison, or death, or permanent misery for the main character, a man who had done bad things.

"Do you really believe that there are some people who are irredeemable?" Michael asked me, moving a branch away from our path.

I thought about what I had been saying—my desire to contain this human in a way that would prevent him from ever causing harm. I had considered my position one about justice—protecting others. Under that metallic sky, walking a bare path with my beloved, I realized the one I wanted to protect was myself, from a world in which bad things happened. Glass my heart.

Raised in the military by a father who taught me that the world was black and white—regulations, chain of command, duty—I had already traded in my Republican belief that reward comes to those who work hard while poverty happens to the lazy—but I realized that wintery morning that I hadn't taken the next step, to believe that no one was beyond love. The heart was bigger than the body in which it roosted.

"I guess not," I said to Michael, surprising myself. Moments before the character had seemed evil to me. Now he appeared only broken.

At that moment a bush to the right of us on the trail exploded in yellow. Hundreds of cedar waxwings took to the sky, lemon-yellow bellies shining brighter than gold amid all that brown and gray.

"Okay," I say to Michael. "Let's not press charges."

When I email Nancy, Michael's sister, later that afternoon to tell her what has happened to Aidan, she writes back immediately.

Her words convey her sadness, even across fifteen hundred miles. She writes, "Hurt people hurt people."

It takes me a while to realize what she means. At first I think she is chanting, "hurt people, hurt people, hurt people," urging me to mama-bear action. But no less generous than her brother, she is really turning my attention to Carson.

"Have you checked to see if they are going to offer him counseling?"

By this point in the day, even after yoga and the Zen story and another conversation with Jen who says, "Your chances of being struck by lightning are greater than those of being in a school shooting," I hate Carson. He poses a threat. So when Nancy asks me if I am following up with the school about counseling for Carson, my response is "What?!"

The Spanish Conquest of Peru, Thirty Years' War, Pequot War, First, Second and Third English Civil Wars, Cromwell's conquest of Ireland, Cromwell's conquest of Scotland, The 335 Years' War, French and Indian Wars, Second Cherokee War, American Revolution, French Revolution, Haitian Revolution, The Napoleonic Wars, The Bolivian War of Independence, Argentine War of Independence, Mexican War of Independence, Venezuelan War of Independence, War of 1812, Columbian, Chilean, Peruvian, and Ecuadorian Wars of Independence, Lower Canada Rebellion, Upper Canada Rebellion, Second Seminole War

Of course, I have already considered the fact that Carson is hit at home. I, and everyone I have told the story to, which at this point stands at half a dozen, all agree that it is significant that Carson slapped Aidan. He didn't punch him. In fact, one of the first questions I asked Aidan when we stopped the car on the yellow brick road was whether he was hit with an open fist or a closed one.

"Why?" Aidan had asked.

And I really couldn't say, except that I had recently learned that in the state of Utah slapping a child is not considered abuse, but hitting them with a closed fist is.

"We have decided as a culture that somehow being hit with an open hand is okay," I tell Aidan. Michael will reaffirm the distinction that night when he asks Aidan the same question upon hearing the story for the first time.

So my guess is that Carson is hit at home, maybe by his mother, given a slap across the face for disagreeing or refusing to eat the dinner she has served. You learn to hit because you are hit. Hurt people hurt people.

"Why do you think he hit you, Aidan?" I asked him the evening after it had happened.

"He was angry?" Aidan responded, clearly uncertain about why he would be hit for disliking football.

"Or maybe he's hit at home and thinks that's how to respond."

"Maybe," Aidan answers, unconvinced.

I know that you can hit your children with an open hand and not be convicted of abuse because I was researching whether I had the obligation to report one of my undergraduates for telling me that he spanked his daughter.

Michael was insistent that I report it, but I was less sure.

The student, Jacob, had been sobbing in my office just a week before Carson slapped Aidan. The Kavanaugh hearings had been scheduled but had not begun. Blasey Ford was saying she might not appear. Her family had been secretly relocated amid an increasing number of death threats. People were threatening to kill her and her family because she stepped forward.

Jacob had emailed me in the midst of this political drama with a subject line that read "Emergency Drop." I didn't know Jacob all that well, never had him as a student before this class, but he had recently left the Church of Jesus Christ of Latter-day Saints and his life was shattered. He had left for his daughter's sake. "So she doesn't have to grow up like I did, so she has choices," he had said one afternoon in my office, sobs bending his body in half.

"I have hurt so many people, Jennifer," he cried then. "I can't live with myself."

Now he emailed to tell me that he had tried to take his own life the night before. That he hated himself and all that he had done. That he had to withdraw from school.

Leaving the Church of Jesus Christ of Latter-day Saints is not like leaving the Episcopal church or even the Catholic church. Especially here in Utah. When you leave, you are cast into outer darkness, a kind of hell reserved for the very worst kind of human, the one who was given the truth and turned his back on it.

You lose everything.

Having lived in Utah for so long, I know scores of students who have left the church—because they were gay, because they didn't believe that only some people were saved, because they uncovered early teachings, because they didn't want to marry and have babies, because they were tired of lying to their parents, to themselves, because they were tired of being told that life must unfold on a singular trajectory. I have sat with many who are grieving over the loss of the life they had been told from birth was the right one to live. These students are so brave, so much braver than I ever was.

In all those conversations, through all those tears, I had never had a student sob for the hurt they had done to others because of their belief system. Like anyone with strongly held convictions, members of the Church of Jesus Christ can be unkind to those outside the church. Not all members. Not all the time. But enough. Jacob had been a good follower, had served well. Of his own admission, he had been the kind of member who was terrible to others. I didn't ask, but I imagined bullying, physically harming, taunting, undermining. I have read lots of essays by students outside the faith tortured in the locker room.

The afternoon after he tried to take his own life, he didn't cry in my office only because of all the harm he had done to others. He also cried because of what he had tried to do to himself. He cried because he was spanking his daughter like his father had him and worried that it would only grow worse as Challis grew older. He cried because he felt imprisoned by his past, that it was making him become all that he hated.

"I am a good father," he told me, his eyes bloodshot and swollen, hair matted and pressed to his head.

I wanted to believe he could change.

That night Michael pressed me to tell someone about Jacob in order to protect myself. I reassured him that Jacob had only spanked Challis, not hit, and he was seeking help.

"Spanking becomes hitting, Jennifer. The line is very murky."

Turns out, in Utah, that particular line is crossed the moment you clench your fist.

I imagine Carson is hit at home.

I hope Challis is not.

Her father was hit by his father.

I have never been hit.

Aidan has been.

I believe that Blasey Ford was prevented from screaming for help when Kavanaugh put his open hand over her mouth.

I have no idea if Kavanaugh has been hit, but I imagine he has been made to feel small.

I have yelled at my sons.

I have yelled at Michael.

I have been kind to others all day long only to release my venom on those I call most dear.

Mormon War, Pastry War, Honey War, First Anglo-Afghan War, First Opium War, The Land Wars, Crimean War, American Civil War, Sioux War, Second Anglo-Afghan War, The Boer Wars, Cuban War of Independence, Spanish-American War, Mexican Revolution, World War I, Russian Revolution, Third Anglo-Afghan War, Irish War of Independence, Afghan Civil War, Japanese Invasion of Manchuria, Saudi-Yemeni War, Spanish Civil War, World War II, Palestine Civil War, Arab-Israeli War, Cold War, Korean War, Cuban Revolution, Tibetan Revolution, Vietnam, Bay of Pigs, Sand War, Laos, Cambodia, The Troubles, Prague Spring, Nicaraguan Revolution

While Blasey Ford studies acute psychological trauma, I spend my days thinking and writing about what I call ordinary trauma. Underneath this essay, I know, rides the question of scale. Aidan was only slapped; Blasey Ford, assaulted; the Jews in World War II, exterminated. These traumas are clearly not the same.

Acute psychological trauma involves an inability to articulate the story of the trauma itself—the trauma haunts the person, refuses to be named, and does its damage by remaining outside the realm of language. But acute psychological trauma is not the only kind of trauma that passes undetected. Ordinary trauma does as well—those events in our life that have the potential to harm but are made, instead, to feel ordinary and therefore to pass unnoticed. I grew up on military bases in the late Cold War when the possibility of nuclear war was ingested with the breakfast cereal. Nuclear annihilation was my constant companion; battleships passed just beyond my backyard. We all experience ordinary trauma; the twenty-four-hour news cycle alone creates a kind of numbness where shootings and beatings become almost mundane. I see hints of ordinary trauma when the counselor tells Aidan that Carson has crossed a line. Boys will be boys.

I think, though, whether considering acute psychological trauma or ordinary trauma, the question of scale is not always the best question to ask. Trauma is not experienced on a universal continuum; it's experienced individually. The irony found in trauma mirrors the irony found in pain. While pain is experienced in isolation, it is universally shared. I cannot know your pain exactly, but we both know pain. A slap is not a shot but both require a shift in the telling of an individual's story about the world.

This past summer, our family drove to Cedar City, Utah, for the Utah Shakespeare Festival. We chose to see two plays: *An Iliad* and *Big River*.

When we arrived, I looked more closely at the plays and realized that *An Iliad* was a one-person play, one person, one stage, for the entire play. When we had originally purchased the tickets, I think we had only noticed the subject matter: ancient Greece and war. We knew the boys, steeped in Percy Jackson, would love it. A one-person production? That seemed like a play without weapons and stage battles and minor explosions. The morning of the performance, I went to the box office to exchange the tickets for something more "accessible." Everything was sold out.

"Would this play be good for my teenage boys?" I asked the ticket person.

"I haven't seen it," he said.

When I got back to the motel, Michael said we should just trust that this was the play we were meant to see and go.

I figured we could buy the boys enough lemon drops to keep them entertained for the ninety-minute production, no intermission.

An Iliad was conceived and written by Lisa Peterson and Denis O'Hare. Shortly after the United States invaded Iraq in 2003, the two playwrights became interested in the question of what it meant to be a country at war. They catalogued all the plays ever written about war and finally arrived at a retelling of Homer's *Iliad*. They chose the epic poem for many reasons, not the least of which being that the story had been handed down orally for generations before being written down by Homer. The story of the Trojan War had traveled from storyteller to storyteller for three thousand years, carried on tongues, in hearts, and finally put to paper.

In their play, the only character is The Poet. The character can be any age, any gender, or any race, but The Poet is the lone speaker of thousands of lines. According to the playwrights, The Poet has been "doomed to tell the story of the Trojan War until the day when human nature changes, when our addiction to rage comes to an end, when the telling of a war story becomes unnecessary." The Poet, who has stood witness to every war waged since the Trojan War, has become "a compendium of war." Under the weight of these stories, he loses himself over the course of the play, deteriorating in front of our eyes, becoming maddened and numbed and frantic with grief. In the climax of the play, The Poet steps forward and begins to name, in order, every war fought since the Trojan War.

Salvadoran Civil War, Soviet Invasion of Afghanistan, Contra war of Nicaragua, Second Sudanese Civil War, Iran-Iraq War, Falklands War, Israeli Invasion of Lebanon, US Invasion of Granada, US Invasion of Panama, First Intifada, Afghan Civil War, Rwandan Civil War, Bosnia and Herzegovina, Chechnya, Afghanistan, Kosovo, Iraq, Chechnya, Afghanistan, Rwanda, Darfur, Iraq, Haiti, Pakistan, Lebanon, Kenya, Zimbabwe, Congo, Gaza, Somalia, Georgia, Iraq, Pakistan, Afghanistan, Libya, Syria*

Aidan and Kellen did not move throughout the play. The four of us sat stunned. Brian Vaughn, who played The Poet, delivered the kind of performance I imagine he had waited his entire life to give. At the moment when he crumples under the "telescopic listing of all wars ever fought," it was all I could do not to rise from my seat, walk onto the stage, and hold him.

When the curtain fell, we were quiet. There was nothing to be said. I have no doubt that the boys will remember that experience for the rest of their lives.

After we returned home, I wrote a letter to Vaughn and tried to express the profundity of our experience, my great thanks for his willingness to give the world such a powerful gift. "If everyone could see you in that play," I wrote him, "the world could change."

Months later, he wrote back, saying he was "tremendously proud" that the show had made such an impression on Aidan and Kellen. "One never knows," he continued, "how a play may impact an audience."

On the day of the Kavanaugh hearings, I spent my morning meditation sending Blasey Ford loving kindness. A fifty-year-old female university professor with blond hair rather than brown, she and I have walked similar paths. I imagine she never asked for this, did not welcome the ways in which her life would forever be changed by stepping forward, but I also imagine she hoped that maybe this time she would be heard. The day after the hearings I sent her my gratitude for her strength, even as I cried with the other women in my Friday morning meditation group. We reassured one another that things were changing, the old was shuddering a dying breath.

It took me a week before I offered my morning meditation to Kavanaugh, not until the Friday at the end of the week in which Aidan had been hit. At first, I could not do it. When I brought his face before me, I could only see the anger, the privilege, the arrogance. So I turned him into a child, not more than five, and wondered what his world was like before he sawed his way through college and law school, before he tasted beer and wine, before he knew rejection, before he first hurt another or was hurt. I imagine that his world, at a very young age, was not all that different from mine, or yours. We come into the world unwounded. And then we learn to wound. With each inhalation, I relished the opportunity we are all given, with every breath, to begin again.

> *As time goes on, it may be necessary to add a war or wars at the end of the list to reflect current events. This should be done with great restraint and include only major conflicts. The same is true of the list of destroyed cities toward the end of the play.

At the end of the school week, I picked Aidan up from school. He came to the car happy, already anticipating the football game that night.

"How was school" I asked. "Anyone hit you today?"

He looked over at me and grinned. "Carson smiled at me in the hallway."

"What did you do?"

"I smiled back."

The Poet does not stand entirely alone on the stage. Early in the play, he calls on The Muse and she arrives. She never speaks. Instead, she plays her violin. Into those notes, saturating the air like the song of a singular bird, uncontained and unbroken, the audience releases their grief, far too heavy to find expression in language.

The playwrights say of their play, "*An Iliad* started out as an examination of war and man's tendency toward war. In the end, it also became an examination of the theater and the way in which we still tell each other stories in order to try to make sense of ourselves, and our behavior."

Both in the play and in our lives, beauty and grace accompany the witness on the journey. Aidan tells me he has been hit. Blasey Ford says she has been assaulted. Jacob says he has hit and been hit. And we all step into a three-thousand-year-old history of war and violence, but also a history of bearing witness, carrying the story, breaking the glass. Things change, things remain the same. We press charges; we don't. We stand on the doorstep and wait for our children to emerge from the yellow school bus. Sometimes we step forward and sometimes we keep silent. Our enemies become our friends and our friends move away. But we keep trying. We keep speaking and writing and sending music into the sky, all in hopes that someday there will no longer be any hurt people to hurt people and the war story might come to an end.

Acknowledgments

When it comes to gratitude, I hope to emulate the ocean, grateful for every river that fills it, humbled by all that arrives. I am thankful to the University of Nebraska Press for believing in this project, especially Alicia Christensen and Courtney Ochsner. My gratitude extends especially to Elizabeth Zaleski, who read the manuscript with such care and attention.

I am also thankful to the literary journals that first published many of these essays, sometimes under different titles, including:

American Scholar: "Headwaters," "Out in the West"
Ascent: "The Little Bear"
Brevity: "Openings," "Running through the Dark"
Colorado Review: "Taxi Sutra"
Creative Nonfiction: "The Wanting Creature"
Ecotone: "Where It is Darkest"
Green Mountains Review: "The Cemetery"
Pilgrimage: "Returned"
Hotel Amerika: "Lobster"

Through the years, I have walked the path with many amazing writers, friends who have given me feedback, encouragement, and, most importantly, love. Those writers include Chris Cokinos, Ben Gunsberg, Debra Gwartney, Mason Jhamb, Rona Kaufman, Kathe Lison, and Charles Waugh. A deep bow to you. Every page is marked by your presence.

I have been equally held in the hearts of so many dear friends, in particular Cathy Best, Chantel Gerfen, Seunghee Ha, Emerson James, Diane Obloch, Richard Owen, Sherrie Mitchell, Jen Peeples, Antra Sinha, and Nancy Sowder.

My gratitude extends to my first source, my parents, Morris and Cynde Sinor, and to my brothers, Scott and Bryan Sinor. They laid the ground for my becoming.

Finally to my husband, the poet Michael Sowder, and my sons, Aidan and Kellen, who, by word and example, return me again and again to this moment, the one right now, which is full and perfect, always and already: "You belong to me, and I am yours."

IN THE AMERICAN LIVES SERIES

To order or obtain more information on these or other University of
Nebraska Press titles, visit nebraskapress.unl.edu.

CPSIA information can be obtained
at www.ICGtesting.com
Printed in the USA
LVHW040551120920
665720LV00006B/692

9 781496 222640